DIVORCE AND REMARRIAGE

DIVORCE AND REMARRIAGE

Towards a New Catholic Teaching

VICTOR J. POSPISHIL

HERDER AND HERDER

1967
HERDER AND HERDER NEW YORK
232 Madison Avenue, New York 10016

CONTENTS

APPENDIXES

DIVORCE AND REMARRIAGE

PREFACE

THAT Christian marriage is indissoluble is a fact undeniably confirmed in the following pages. If the Church has been throughout the past centuries so very understanding, so clement and compassionate towards the innocent husband or wife whose home was irreparably broken up, and if she has exercised her redeeming authority received from Christ by permitting in certain cases the dissolution of a bond which she, the Church, had always known and wanted to be indissoluble, the reader of this book will nevertheless realize after examining the facts and texts quoted by the author how very reluctant the Church has been every time she found herself compelled to consent to an exception to a law in which she found her strength and her pride. Sometimes obliged to take into account human weakness and consequently to forsake her intransigence for fear of losing a soul, the Church militant suffers from having "to eat and drink with the publicans and sinners" who compose it and who are, in truth, the very *raison d'être* of her existence. She suffers from having to adapt herself continually to men made of flesh and blood, and she aspires with St. Paul to find herself some day delivered from "the body of this death" (Rom. 7, 24). Nevertheless, this suffering is inherent to the life of the Church which does not wish to be triumphant among her own children who lead a life of pain and struggle.

No sooner had the press diffused my first intervention before the Council in favor of the innocent husband or wife (October 29, 1965) than a great number of messages from all parts of the world arrived conveying to me with their pathetic expression of satisfaction and gratitude a description of the sufferings of deserted husbands and wives and of the anxiety of their pastors. I was thus able to collect, apart from the argument of the pastoral, scriptural, theological, or historical order invoked by men of the Church and other specialists, numerous reflections from clearly well-intentioned believers which bore the marks of their spontaneity of feeling and of their straightforward common sense.

Some of my correspondents wondered whether it was fair for the innocent party to be placed under the obligation of spending the rest of his or her life repairing the sin of the other spouse in a solitude for which neither of them was intended.

Others found it simply immoral that the abandoned innocent party would be so debased as to wish the death of the deserter—this being the only means for regaining freedom and starting a new life. There is the typical case of a good man who seemed to regret having saved his wife from certain death, because the woman, once recovered, deserted him to contract a new union. He said in his letter to me: "It is because I saved her from death that I am now condemned to my present solitude which is bound to last as long as she lives."

Still other correspondents considered it to be far from evangelical that Catholic moralists would tend to let the abandoned innocent partner spiritually perish—by condemning him to remain exposed in most cases to a serious risk of perdition—under the pretext of protecting the large majority of believers against possible abuse of the law.

My correspondents regarded such tendency as being scarcely compatible with the spirit of the Gospel parable of the good shepherd who seeks out the lost sheep, while forgetting for a time the other ninety-nine.

I may remark here that all those moralists can fear is a "possible" abuse. In fact, if cases of divorce have registered in recent years a certain increase in our dechristianized society where little or no consideration is given to the laws of the Church, the situation of married couples among believers is altogether different. Although divorce is admitted by the non-Catholic Churches of the East, we can testify that the family bond among the communities dependent on these Churches is as stable and as sacred as in the most Catholic communities of the West. Divorce in the non-Catholic Churches of the East is the exception, exactly as are declarations of nullity of marriage among Catholics.

In connection with this particular point, some of my correspondents remarked that they cannot discern a difference between true divorce and the declaration of nullity granted— after ten, twenty, or more years of common life, spent in peace, resignation, or even relative happiness—on such grounds as defects in the form, spiritual relationship, and physical or moral compulsion. Others declared that they simply do not understand these "annulments" of marriage and prefer a simple and frank dispensation from the matrimonial bond to be granted as an exception to the innocent husband or wife who, as a result of being deserted by his or her partner, has no other alternative but to contract a legitimate marriage or to slide into perdition.

I have given just a few examples of the judicious and by no means negligible reflections culled at random from my voluminous and profoundly humane correspondence.

To be sure, Monsignor Pospishil has in no way reduced in his book the indissolubility of marriage to a problem of pure exegesis. Whatever might be the interpretation given to the text of St. Matthew (19, 9), we must admit that there does exist an ecclesiastical tradition of tolerance, clear and venerable like every other tradition of the Church, which was accepted and practiced by many holy Fathers of the East and of the West.

The East has always followed this tradition of tolerance and has remained faithful to it. The West maintained it for many centuries with the positive approval of many of its bishops, popes, and councils, and in fact never attempted to condemn it in the East, even after the cessation of its practice in the West. We may recall here the decision purposely taken by the Council of Trent to amend the formula which this Council was preparing to adopt, because, as was said by Monsignor Guerrero, then the Archbishop of Granada, the Church cannot condemn the holy doctors of the Church: *"Non placet igitur quod sancti Doctores damnentur."*

According to this tradition, the Church, unanimously asserting the principle of the indissolubility of Christian marriage, did in the past as it now does in the East believe in her right of dispensation in certain cases from the matrimonial bond, and she has in fact often granted this dispensation as an act of necessary tolerance in the pastoral field.

Therefore, there can be no question in the present era of openness and dialogue of denying the legitimacy of a two-thousand-year-old discipline which still remains in force in the oriental, orthodox half of the Christian world.

The author has the well-deserved merit of his success in collecting and placing before the conscience of the Church the evidence of so many centuries of pastoral tolerance. By no means has he the intention of combatting the indissolubility of marriage. On the contrary, he vigorously asserts it as being a universal doctrine of the Church. But, he wants also to show that God, who instituted marriage, can alone dissolve it by His own authority and that the Church, which perpetuates Jesus Christ on earth, can do it by virtue of this same authority. And the Church has done it.

It was urgent on the eve of engaging in the dialogue between Churches to recall this tradition which the Christian East cannot renounce without condemning itself. The future generations will bless Monsignor Pospishil for having placed in evidence this tradition of tolerance and thus contributing to the progress of the ecumenical dialogue.

It belongs to the Church, it is in fact her duty, to give a pastoral, an adequate, and an authentic interpretation to so imposing and durable a tradition.

✟ *Elias Zoghby*

14

INTRODUCTION

SOME of those who read the title of this book may suspect that it is an attempt to challenge a securely established teaching of the Catholic Church. They would not be wrong in regarding the indissolubility of a consummated, sacramental marriage a part of Catholic doctrine, because it was so considered for centuries by the theologians of the Western Catholic Church. Therefore, before one contests the theological characteristics assigned to this dogmatic proposition, it will be indispensable to explain how any Catholic teaching is established within the theological system of the Church.

The first and most important source of any teaching in the Church is the word of God, divine revelation, as it is preserved for us in the Bible. However, since the exact meaning of a certain passage of sacred Scripture might not be obvious and therefore will have been subjected to varying explanations over the centuries—although the Church has perhaps now accepted one of them as the only true—it is necessary also to study the witness of tradition. Not all that Jesus did or said was recorded (Jn. 21, 23); much was preserved for posterity in the teaching and daily practice of the early Church, and was further developed by the Fathers. To this must be added the opinions of ecclesiastical gatherings, synods and councils, and the decisions and pronouncements of the ecclesiastical hierarchy, chiefly of the Roman pontiffs. This witness of the past will usually suffice to prove that the sense of a certain passage in sacred Scripture is to be understood according to the teaching the Church has accepted as the true and divinely revealed one.

Catholic theology finds another instrument for the elucidation of doctrine in human reason. Although the immortality of the soul, to give an example, is clearly taught in Scripture and tradition, insights derived from philosophical speculation enlarge the evidence justifying the teaching of the Church.

If a certain doctrine has been challenged either by groups inside the Church, as for example those who opposed the teaching of papal infallibility, or by groups on the outside, such as the exponents of materialistic communism, the Church might decide to precision a specific teaching by a magisterial pronouncement, of which various degrees are possible, from the highest, a dogmatic definition, to a simple *monitum* of the Sacred Congregation for the Teaching of the Faith (Holy Office).

In respect to the question of the dissolubility of consummated, sacramental marriages, it is now the official teaching of the Catholic Church that such marriages cannot be dissolved by any authority on earth. This dogmatic proposition has the theological qualification of a *propositio proxima fidei*. It is not the aim of this study to contradict directly this doctrine, but rather to show that all marriages *can be dissolved* on earth, that divine authority is required for this, and that the Catholic Church possesses such power.

It is therefore submitted that:

(1) Sacred Scripture, that is, the New Testament, does not teach the impossibility of total divorce when such divorce is granted by the Church in virtue of her divine authority. Thus the distinction is made here between *intrinsic* dissolubility, that is, when the spouses themselves are legally entitled to dissolve the marriage contract, and *extrinsic* dissolubility, that is, when some authority outside the marriage partners, as God, the Church, the state, can dissolve the marriage. According to the laws of God, of the Church, and of most religions and states, marriage is intrinsically indissoluble. In respect to extrinsic indissolubility, all other major religious denominations, nations, and states permit divorce and remarriage, and it is only the Catholic Church which maintains at the present time that sacramental marriages, that is, marital unions between baptized persons, cannot be dissolved for any reasons whatsoever except by death.

This book treats solely the problem of extrinsic dissolubility to be effected or denied exclusively by the Catholic Church.

(2) Tradition, including the Fathers, synods, and other

legislative documents of the Christian East as well as of the West, taken as a whole, is not sufficiently clear to decide this question, although a distinct majority of the Fathers and ancient ecclesiastical authorities permitted the remarriage of husbands of adulterous wives, while generally denying it to all wives, even the innocent.

(3) The pronouncements of the Council of Trent in this matter do not resolve the issue.

(4) Whatever rational grounds are proffered by Catholic theologians for excluding some kinds of divorces can be matched by at least equally valid and even more powerful reasons for assigning to the Church the authority to grant complete divorce of sacramental marriages.

It is proposed, in sum, that the Catholic Church recognize that she possesses from her divine Founder the unlimited power of the keys, the authority to grant total divorce and to permit the remarriage of divorced Christians.

The author is fully aware that these pages contain a mere general outline of their thesis. Each part of the book would require a separate treatment before it could be stated with assurance that the thesis has been proved; and it is far from the mind of the author to imply that the final word has been said on the problem. Nor can there be any doubt that it is the official teaching of the Catholic Church at the present time that a Christian consummated marriage is absolutely indissoluble. But a majority of the theologians who have studied the problem agree that this doctrine is not defined *de fide*. This means for all practical purposes that a Catholic is obliged in his conscience to give his internal assent to this teaching. It does not, however, preclude the possibility that such a teaching might be changed. Thus Tanquerey says in respect to such doctrines that "if all theologians teach a certain doctrine, which by its nature refers to faith or morals, as true and certain, it would be temerity to reject it, unless new proofs, heretofore unknown to the theologians, have come up." [1]

1. *Synopsis Theologicae Dogmaticae,* vol. I, p. 664.

Modern scientific studies in various fields have admitted working hypotheses or provisional assumptions which later were proved to be incorrect. But in the interim they were useful because of the stimulus they created in the way of directing the efforts of students towards a new solution. The privilege of a working hypothesis is claimed for the present proposal. It is felt that this is a duty and a right because, as Karl Rahner has remarked, "the individual within the Church must be allowed to address the Church community in general as a publicist—not only to make direct representations to the hierarchy," [2] and that "ultimately it all boils down to the fact that every individual Christian is responsible in his own day and way for the Church and the life of the Church." [3]

If anything new is here propounded, it is offered not as the ultimate and final solution, but as a mere attempt in the direction of finding the truth, subject to correction not only by those who know better and are able to refute it with more cogent arguments or proofs, but also by the authority of the Church. After all, if we are seeking here to assign to the Church a power and authority which contemporary theologians generally deny to her, the ultimate decision must be left to the magisterium of the Church herself.

2. *Free Speech in the Church*, p. 27.
3. *Ibid.*, p. 50.

I.

DIVORCE IN THE BIBLE

1. INTRODUCTORY REMARKS

THE Old and the New Testament refer in a few places to divorce. But it must be stated at once that the meaning of these passages is not clear. If it were, there would never have developed differences of opinion on this question, and no synod or council would have felt it necessary to make official pronouncements on the problem.

This last remark cannot be sufficiently repeated because to many a Catholic it seems that holy Scripture has spoken quite clearly and definitely, and has excluded any possibility of a total divorce of the bond of sacramental marriages. If, then, anyone advances the possibility that the meaning of these passages might not be so unequivocal, an emotional defensive remonstrance is usually aroused. However, as in so many other instances, the true meaning of certain passages of the Bible will be open to us only if we have recourse to the interpretation offered to us by the Fathers of the Church. They, being so much nearer to the time of the writing of the Gospels, and being often the recipients of oral traditions handed down to them from the apostles, are presumed to have an insight into Holy Writ lacking to a later age. But when Patristic evidence is limited, or not yet developed fully, or not unanimous but evenly distributed over the entire gamut of possible interpretations, then the authority of the Church will have to be approached for a solution.

As we shall see, an analysis of the pertinent texts from the Old and New Testaments does not lead us to any unequivocal decision. From the fact that the Fathers were not able to arrive at a unanimous opinion of the meaning of the relevant

Scripture passages, and that Christians of the East and of the West are divided today on this score, we must infer that it will always be impossible to settle the problem by reference to holy Scripture and tradition alone. One is therefore driven to conclude again that a final judgment can be arrived at solely with the aid of the official teaching authority of the Church.

It would be pointless, then, if one were to try to attempt to resolve the problem with finality by these biblical texts, since one cannot presume to achieve a higher degree of certainty than was attainable by the preceding two millenniums of Christianity. Of course, the number of Catholic authors who made and continue to make attempts to bring the question to a definitive solution is quite large—but they do this in the face of the insurmountable obstacle of a divided and irreconcilable exegetical past. Thus it is somewhat incomprehensible to read a statement as that of Alberto Vaccari, S. J., professor in the Pontifical Institute in Rome, who first tried to interpret the words of Matthew 19, 9, by analyzing two terms, the Greek expressions for adultery (*moikheia*) and fornication (*porneia*), while failing to mention the occasion and circumstances in which Jesus uttered them, and who, second, concludes from this linguistic study "that any shadow of doubt about the indissolubility of marriage is forever dispelled." [1]

There is a Latin saying that who proves too much proves nothing, and this applies to all such similar conclusions. The truth is that the several references in holy Scripture to divorce can be understood differently from the prevailing Catholic teaching, and have been so understood by holy, learned, and dedicated Churches and saints, as well as by theologians of the past and present.

While it is denied that the permission of divorce can be inferred from holy Scripture alone, it is also maintained that neither can the opposite doctrine be established exclusively from the Gospels and St. Paul's writings. L. Housman, C.Ss.R. and A. van der Born have rightly noted "that most of the

1. "Divorce in the Gospels," pp. 31–33.

20

attempts to arrive at such a harmonious interpretation are far from satisfactory exegetically. What can be called the 'common' interpretation among Catholics is the one which sees in the 'exceptive' clauses the right of an injured husband to have a 'separation from bed and board' from an adulterous wife, but without the right of remarriage. This may be good theology, but it is poor exegesis, for violence must be done to the texts to make them mean that." [2]

Similarly, A. Ott in his monograph on this topic observes "that no strict proof for absolute indissolubility can be deduced from passages of Paul, for the exception is simply not mentioned." [3]

It would therefore not clarify the matter if we should try to propose a new biblical interpretation as the final solution; rather, we intend simply to reexamine the texts in the light of the two following aims:

(1) The assurance of recognized Catholic biblical scholars of our times will be accepted that these passages in the Bible cannot be interpreted by assuming *a priori* that they are a proof for the absolute indissolubility of marriage.

(2) Other possible explanations will be advanced differing from those commonly accepted by Catholic theologians. These interpretations, which reflect largely the tradition of the Eastern Churches, will not be submitted as final conclusions, but only as theoretically possible hypotheses, to be studied, rejected, or accepted by enlightened scholarship.

2. THE TEXTS

Every translation of holy Scripture will indicate the doctrinal persuasion of the translator.[1] In the present case, the differ-

---

2. "Divorce," in *Encyclopedic Dictionary of the Bible*, p. 582.
3. *Die Auslegung der neutestamentlichen Texte über die Ehescheidung, historisch, kritisch dargestellt*, p. 157.
1. An example of purposeful, though wellmeaning bias is Jerome's translation of the story of Onan (Gen. 38, 8–10). John T. Noonan

ences will depend on whether a given translator believes that divorce is permitted or not. He cannot avoid this bias, since the original Greek text was ambiguous. It is important to underline this fact for the benefit not only of the laity, but also the majority of the clergy, who could easily wonder why there is any question raised at all, since the text, read in a translation, seems so "clear" and "self-evident."

The pertinent passages from the New Testament found here are taken from the *Revised Standard Version* (Catholic Edition),[2] because it is now accepted by Protestants and Catholics alike, and there is thus a reasonable presumption that it seeks to render the texts without confessional bias.

In addition to the texts to be examined shortly, there are a few others—such as that of St. Paul on the possibility of divorce and remarriage for a Christian from his or her unbelieving spouse—which have been omitted because they do not concern the present topic.

3. THE METHOD OF BIBLICAL INTERPRETATION

In exploring the meaning of a statement found in any literary document, especially one from remote times, we will be bound by the general principles of literary and historical criticism. Thus the exegete must avoid reading into Scripture a sense which will support a certain teaching of his own Church. Only after he has established the meaning by independent and unbiased study can he pass his interpretation on to the theologian, whose task it will be to relate the specific passage to a dogmatic synthesis.

Some Catholic theologians have sought to avoid the dis-

---

concludes that the passage was changed to sound much more severe than in the original: "It incorporated Jerome's judgment of the practice" (*Contraception. A History of its Treatment by the Catholic Theologians and Canonists,* p. 102).

2. New York and Edinburgh, 1966.

crepancies among several passages in the New Testament referring to divorce by simply ignoring those which are not in conformity with their argumentation. R. Souarn, to take an example, justifies this method of scholarly investigation by asserting that each Gospel is complete in itself and independent from other parts of the New Testament.[1] It is difficult to see how this can be reconciled with the dogmatic proposition that Scripture needs to be complemented by a non-written source, the tradition of the Church, in accord with the statement of John 21, 25, that "there are also many other things which Jesus did; were every one of them to be written, I suppose that the world itself could not contain the books that would be written."

In studying the meaning of some passages of Scripture, there should be no difference between a Catholic and a Protestant student of the Bible, because both ought to be guided solely by the scientific principles established in this branch of sacred science. The attitude of a number of Catholic exegetes when they discuss the passages in the New Testament that refer to divorce is one of defense. They interpret the Gospel according to text and context, but whenever a doubt arises they apply a corrective, namely, their understanding of the present doctrine of Catholic theology and canon law. Therefore, what they accomplish is not an independent biblical inquiry but an accommodation of holy Scripture to the—perhaps true, perhaps assumed—requirements of contemporary theology.

4. BIBLICAL REFERENCES TO DIVORCE

The various passages in the Old and New Testament referring to divorce, separation, and remarriage cannot be understood without making that fundamental distinction between intrinsic

1. "Les Grecs objectent que l'écrivain sacré laissait aux autres évangélistes, le soin de completer, mais il faut répondre que chaque Evangile forme un tout complet et indépendant des autres livres du Nouveau Testament" ("L'adultère et le lien du mariage d'après l'Ecriture Sainte," in *Dictionnaire de Théologie Catholique,* vol. II, col. 470).

and extrinsic dissolubility or indissolubility which we discussed above.

The student of passages of Scriptures will have to search in each instance whether a given passage refers to intrinsic or extrinsic dissolubility, or perhaps to both.[1] According to present Catholic teaching, a sacramental, consummated marital union is intrinsically and extrinsically indissoluble. We can say at once that this absolute indissolubility cannot be based first on the sacramental character alone, because the Church does dissolve sacramental marriages, namely, those which have not been sexually consummated, or second, on the consummation alone, because the Church does dissolve valid natural or non-sacramental marriages, even when entered in the Church, although they are consummated. Therefore, if sacramental marriages are indissoluble, it must be on the grounds of both elements, that is, sacramentality and consummation.[2]

5. THE OLD TESTAMENT ON DIVORCE

Because the New Testament often refers to the Old Testament on this question, it is necessary first to analyze these passages of the latter. One can say at once that Jesus understood the Mosaic legislation concerning the dissolution of marriage in the following senses: (1) that the ideal and original state knew no dissolubility of marriage ("but from the beginning it was not so"); (2) that there is absolute intrinsic indissolubility of any and every marriage ("what God has joined together let no man put asunder"); and (3) that extrinsic dissolution was permitted for one reason only: adultery, or separation of the wife and bodily affiliation with another man. Dissolution was

1. We are following in this analysis of biblical references to divorce the ideas expressed by William R. O'Connor in "The Indissolubility of a Ratified, Consummated Marriage," in *Ephemerides Theologicae Lovanienses,* pp. 692–722.
2. F. M. Cappello, *De Matrimonio,* n. 755.

not enjoined as an obligation, as we find it in certain passages of the Old Testament, and forgiveness of the transgression was counselled, because God granted such divorces solely "by reason of the hardness of your heart." As far as Christ's understanding of the Mosaic law went, therefore, we can conclude with William R. O'Connor that "there is nowhere in the Gospels an absolute prohibition of all dissolubility, extrinsic as well as intrinsic for all cases of marriage." [3]

O'Connor also emphasizes the twofold character of the law of Moses: the *toleration* of divorce, and the *command* to observe certain formalities in obtaining it.[4] St. Thomas himself already emphasized that two things were *permitted* in the law of Moses: (1) dismissal of the wife by the husband; and (2) remarriage of the wife to another man, excepting a priest (Lev. 21, 14); while two conditions were *demanded:* (1) the issuance of a writ of divorce (*libellum repudii*) according to strict procedural formalities, and (2) absolute prohibition of the woman to return to the dismissing husband.[5] This distinction between what was permissible and what was obligatory finds expression in the two following Old Testament passages referred to in the conversation of the Pharisees with Jesus.[6]

Genesis 1, 27: *And God created man to his own image, to the image of God he created him; male and female he created them.*

Genesis 2, 24: *For this reason a man shall leave his father and mother and be joined to his wife, and the two shall become one.*

Of these passages adduced by Jesus two questions can be asked. First, does this refer to all marriages without the dis-

3. *Art. cit.,* p. 713.
4. *Ibid.,* p. 704.
5. *Commentary on the Sentences,* IV, dist. 33, q. 2, a. 2; q. 4, s. 4.
6. Mt. 19, 7: "Why then did Moses *command* one to give a writ of divorce . . . ?"; Mt. 19, 8: "He said to them, ' . . . *Moses allowed* you . . . "; Mk. 10, 3: "He answered them, 'What did Moses *command* you?' "; Mk. 10, 4: "They said, 'Moses *allowed* . . . ' "

tinctions we presently make? Does it forbid intrinsic as well as extrinsic divorce, or both?

It is clear that one cannot restrict the meaning to consummated sacramental marriages because at the time these words were uttered there was only one kind of marriage. Adam and Eve could have understood them solely with reference to their own and similar unions. Moreover, the Old Testament knew of but one kind of marriage, and therefore it must be assumed that this principle applies also to all present-day marriages. However, if it is thus a general axiom excluding divorce in respect to all marital unions, it can refer only to intrinsic dissolubility, that is, that the marriage cannot be dissolved by the partners themselves. The passage says nothing whatever concerning extrinsic dissolubility. When the words in Genesis were uttered there was only one pair of human beings and only one marriage in existence. Obviously, there could be no reference to divorce and consequent possibility of remarriage if there were no other man or woman available for remarriage. Also, Adam and Eve were in the state of innocence, not yet subject to concupiscence, and there was simply no temptation to divorce.

Gigot admits that there was no possibility for divorce-remarriage when God is said to have made this statement, but he is wrong in concluding: "Plainly then, in making as he did the first human pair, God did not allow divorce." [7] O'Connor rightly corrects this by making the distinction: " 'God did not allow divorce' might perhaps be a little more exact if it read: 'God did not provide for divorce.' Intrinsic dissolubility was excluded by the circumstances of the case . . . Extrinsic dissolubility, too, was not provided for as something altogether unnecessary and unbecoming the state of innocence and integrity in which the first human pair was founded. Was it also excluded in the same way that intrinsic dissolubility was excluded? We do not think so; on the contrary, there seems to be nothing against the

7. *Christ's Teaching Concerning Divorce in the New Testament*, p. 192, n. 1.

possibility of extrinsic dissolubility in the account of the institution of marriage in Genesis. The parties indeed to the marriage may not take it upon themselves to dissolve the contract precisely because God is also concerned in it: there is nothing however to prevent God himself from authorizing and permitting the dissolution." [8]

Therefore, the passage of Genesis 1, 27, is to be understood as a general establishment of the institution of marriage, as a pronouncement of the ideal marriage, and at the most as a prohibition of intrinsic dissolubility, that is, that effected by the marriage partners independently of God's authority.

Deuteronomy 24, 1–4

When a man takes a wife and marries her, if then she finds no favor in his eyes because he has found some indecency ['ervath dabhar] in her, and he writes her a bill of divorce and puts it in her hand and sends her out of his house, and she departs out of his house, and if she goes and becomes another man's wife, and the latter husband dislikes her and writes her a bill of divorce and puts it in her hand and sends her out of his house, or if the latter husband dies, who took her to be his wife, then her former husband, who sent her away, may not take her again to be his wife, after she has been defiled; for that is an abomination before the Lord . . .

Deuteronomy 24, 1–4, is a permission of divorce. It was a recognition of the general custom in vogue by all the peoples surrounding Israel, and also by the Israelites themselves. This authority granted to the husband is to be viewed as an extrinsic dissolution, effected by divine authority but exercised by the husband.

A case of divorce in the Bible prior to Moses is that of Agar from Abraham as related in Genesis 21, 9–14. Sarah had no son and at her request Abraham married her servant Agar (Gen. 16, 1–3). The moral and legal character of Abraham's and Agar's union is also indicated by two other considerations,

8. *Art cit.*, p. 699.

namely, that God would not permit the institution of sexual unions outside of marriage, and that he intervened in its dissolution. After the birth of Isaac, Sarah wished to rid the family of Agar's son Ishmael, and Abraham dismissed Agar after he had received special authorization from God (Gen. 21, 11–12). This dismissal can be regarded as an extrinsic dissolution of the marriage by virtue of God's intervention.

Deuteronomy 24, 1–4, forbade a husband to remarry his divorced wife if she had had in the meantime a relationship with another man, for example by being married to him and then divorced. The grounds for divorcing her in the first place, *'ervath dabhar,* is translated as something indecent, unclean, nakedness of a thing. This obscure phrase was later interpreted with varying degrees of stringency. The school of Rabbi Shammai permitted the husband to divorce his wife solely for serious misconduct, of which adultery was the gravest. Rabbi Hillel's school authorized divorce for any physical or moral defect, even, for example, a spoiled sauce or a burned roast. Rabbi Aqiba went even further by stating that it would be enough for a husband that he should find his wife uglier or less attractive than another woman.[9]

6. THE NEW TESTAMENT ON DIVORCE

The most important text on divorce is in the Gospel according to Matthew (ch. 19) because it contains the significant clause "except for unchastity."

"Is it lawful to divorce one's wife for any cause?" (*v. 3*).
It is clear that the Pharisees wished to hear a solution to the problem raised by the differences among the various rabbinical schools concerning the meaning of *'ervath dabhar.* It is not necessary to assume that they wished to lay a snare for Jesus

9. F. Prat, *Jesus Christ, His Life, His Teaching, and His Work,* vol. II, pp. 79–81.

because whatever he replied would still be within the boundaries of admissible Jewish interpretation. Yet, they probably expected him to disavow the lax teachings of Rabbis Hillel and Aqiba.

". . . the two shall become one" (*v. 5*)

This reference to Genesis 2, 24, as we have seen, is a clear expression of intrinsic indissolubility. "He saw that the current laxity was going far beyond the extrinsic dissolubility recognized by Deuteronomy and was endangering the intrinsic indissolubility that is attached to every marriage, whether it be extrinsically dissoluble or not." [1] In order to confirm the intrinsic indissolubility, Jesus quotes the tradition of the original institution of marriage, and adds to it his reminder that marriage is not a private contract, subject entirely to the will of the partners, but rather a divine institution in which God's action intervenes in every instance: "What therefore God has joined together, let no man put asunder" (v. 6). The expression "the two shall become one" does not exclude the possibility of extrinsic dissolubility, unless we would assume that God excluded extrinsic dissolubility of marriage in principle, and that every marriage is indissoluble. However, since neither in the Old Testament nor in the present economy all marriages are indissoluble, therefore no inference can be drawn in respect to extrinsic indissolubility or dissolubility.

". . . let no man put asunder" (*v. 6; see Mk. 10, 9*)

Does this refer to intrinsic or extrinsic dissolubility or to both? If one were to assume that this is a condemnation of dissolubility in general and of all its forms, then how could one justify the dissolutions the Church permits or grants today: Pauline Privilege and Privilege of the Faith, and of non-consummated sacramental marriages?

It seems inadmissible to assume that Jesus gave a reply of

---

1. O'Connor, *art. cit.,* p. 697.

this meaning to the Pharisees, by referring solely to consummated sacramental marriages, since first he would have spoken of a kind of marriage that did not exist as yet, and therefore this answer would have not been understandable either to the Jews or to the apostles; second, he would not have responded at all to the question of the Pharisees with reference to the differences between the rabbinical schools; and third, he referred to Genesis 1, 27, and 2, 24, thus clearly showing that he spoke of every marriage or of marriage in general. It would follow that all marriages are equally indissoluble. But this can be accepted only as long as it is limited to intrinsic indissolubility.

One can conclude, therefore, that what Jesus meant was that man has no right as such to dissolve a marriage because God is the author of the institution and he is included in every marriage contract. In other words, private authority is insufficient for the termination of marriage. Nothing was said concerning extrinsic dissolubility—which needs authorization from God—since the husband possessed this right at the time of Jesus, provided he exercised it solely within the scope of the law of God. This teaching indirectly excluded the application of all the doctrines of the various rabbinical schools, and restricted divorce to one sole ground, the total separation of the spouses effected definitively by the sexual union of the wife with another man, that is, adultery.

"Why then did Moses command one to give a certificate of divorce . . . ?" (v. 7)
The Pharisees continued their questioning only now focusing on the problem of extrinsic dissolubility allowed in the Mosaic law. Actually, Moses did not inaugurate divorce as such, because it existed before him in all surrounding nations, and it was also permissible among the Israelites. Moses made it a legal institution by assigning limits to it, although they were too vaguely defined because the expression "something indecent" (*'ervath dabhar*), as we have seen, was open to a very loose

interpetation. In addition, certain formalities were prescribed which had to be observed by the husband. Legal grounds, procedural formalities, and the watchful eyes of a tightly knit community were in the beginning a sufficient barrier against abuse of this power by husbands. Also, the more extensive practice of polygamy during the centuries of warfare with the Philistines, Canaanites, and other peoples in Palestine reduced the need for divorce. The temptation to abuse increased at later times and led to an entire gamut of alleged justifications for divorce.

"For your hardness of heart Moses allowed you to divorce your wives, but from the beginning it was not so" (v. 8)

In this passage Jesus explicitly states that Moses gave to the husband the right of divorcing his wife. This is his reply to the original question in verse 3, "Is it lawful to divorce one's wife for *any cause?"* The Pharisees were inquiring about a law in force in their times the interpretation of which was disputed. Jesus' answer refers to the meaning of *'ervath dabhar.* There were three possible interpretations.

First, there was one which put no limit whatever to the authority of the husband, as exemplified by the teaching of the schools of Hillel and Aqiba. This virtually abolished intrinsic indissolubility, and was therefore excluded by Jesus with reference to Genesis. A second permitted dismissal of the wife, in addition to adultery, also for other serious indecencies— according to the teaching of Rabbi Shammai. St. Thomas was of the opinion that *'ervath dabhar* referred not so much to a defilement of sin, but rather a legal defilement, such as contracted by touching a corpse or a leper.[2] This interpretation can be considered within the law at the time of Jesus, but this, as we shall see, was changed by him.[3]

2. III, q. 67, a. 4, ad 5.
3. We must therefore reject the objection of J. Mc Rory that this explanation of Matthew 19 seems to imply that Jesus' interpretation of the meaning of the law did not go beyond that proposed by Rabbi

The third interpretation recognized only adultery as a valid ground for divorce. This is what Jesus established here, for he declared in Matthew 5, 17–18, that he did not come to abolish the law, but to fulfill it.

The differences between these three schools referred solely to the legality of the writ of divorce, not to its validity. The schools wished to establish moral norms for husbands who intended to divorce a wife. To act contrary to these norms would have meant sin, but this would not have affected the validity of the writ of divorce. "It was the intention of neither school to restrict the husband's legal power of divorcing his wife; they differed merely in their moral judgment on divorce." [4] This is important for the understanding of the discussion between Jesus and the Pharisees, and between Jesus and the apostles. We can assume that they did not question whether the husband *could,* legally speaking, divorce his wife, but whether he *should,* and under what conditions. The husband's conduct and not his legal right were the topic of discussion. Consequently, the disapproval of divorce voiced by Jesus would not imply an absolute prohibition of divorce and remarriage.

> ". . . *whoever divorces his wife, except for unchastity, and marries another, commits adultery*" (*v.* 9)
> ". . . *every one who divorces his wife, except on the ground of unchastity, makes her an adulteress; and whoever marries a divorced woman commits adultery*" (*Mt. 5, 32*)

Here Jesus spoke of the wife who had not been divorced within the limits of the law, namely, for adultery. Practically speaking, she had no way of livelihood unless she were ac-

---

Shammai (*The New Testament and Divorce,* p. 49). Shammai knew more grounds for divorce than adultery alone, and Jesus revoked them, leaving adultery as the sole ground.

4. Yaron, "The Jewish Law of Divorce at the Time of the New Testament," in *Marriage Breakdown, Divorce, Remarriage. A Christian Understanding,* p. 57.

cepted into the household of another man, and this normally could be done only by attempting marriage to him. Jesus "was not here introducing a new law, but correcting the abuses of an old law and restoring it to its original intent for those who were still subject to it: it was an interpretation—the only true interpretation—that he gave, and not a promulgation." [5] Many have seen in these words of Jesus an abrogation of the law of Moses permitting extrinsic dissolution or divorce. But again it must be asked: If this were true, how can we explain that these marriages, that is, non-sacramental, natural marital unions, are capable of being dissolved by the Church?

Rather, one can assume that Jesus reaffirmed intrinsic indissolubility and reestablished the true *ideal* of marriage which excludes also extrinsic dissolubility. However, the ideal should not be extended to the point of excluding all extrinsic dissolutions because, after all, God himself permitted them (Deut. 24).

"If such is the case of a man with his wife, it is not expedient to marry" (Mt. 19, 10–11; see Mk. 10, 11–13)

In determining the meaning of the apostles' question and Jesus' reply we must inquire if they had reference to intrinsic only or also to extrinsic dissolubility.

Although absolute indissolubility, including intrinsic and extrinsic indissolubility, would seem the most obvious explanation of the meaning of this passage, this must be rejected. If the topic was extrinsic indissolubility, then it would have embraced all marriages and one could not explain why the Church can dissolve some of them, namely, any natural marriage or consummated sacramental marriages. Only if one restricts the prohibition to intrinsic dissolubility, effected by the partners themselves, would it be true that "whoever divorces his wife . . . and marries another, commits adultery." However, when the husband made use of the writ of divorce against an adulterous wife—and the Church in the case of all marriages—the

5. O'Connor, *art. cit.*, p. 707.

marriage bond is dissolved by divine authority exercised through human instruments, namely, in the Old Testament by the husband, and in the New Testament by the Church.

The bewilderment of the apostles, still at the beginning of their religious mission and imbued with the spirit of their environment, can be explained in other terms. They could quite well have understood that adultery of the wife constituted a sufficient ground for divorce. However, among the Jews of that epoch, still a predominantly agricultural society, adultery of a married woman must have been rather infrequent, while there might be other cogent reasons for wishing to divorce a wife, such as those advanced in many contemporary divorce suits. If only adultery was a ground for divorce, then, practically speaking, there was no divorce at all, and then it seemed to the apostles better not to be married at all than possibly be fettered to a bad wife. Jesus restored their peace of mind by advancing an entirely new idea, voluntary celibacy. Thus, nobody was forced to a celibate life if he adhered to the law, and if he had divorced his wife for adultery.

". . . the husband should not divorce his wife" (*1 Cor. 7,* 11)

Here St. Paul undoubtedly speaks of the sacramental marriage of two Christians. However, the principle he establishes, which excludes separation or divorce, is not his, but is referred to Jesus. Since Jesus' teaching in the various passages of the Gospels (Mt. 5, 32; 19, 9; Mk. 10, 9; Lk. 16, 18) concerns only intrinsic indissolubility, the same can be affirmed of the teaching of Paul. We cannot go so far as to say that thereby the apostle permitted extrinsic dissolubility, but neither can it be affirmed that he excluded the possibility. The high moral standards of the Christian community would have made mention of the possibility of divorce between two baptized believers incongruous, but it was not the same with regard to the marriages of believers with non-believers. Here the difference of religious outlook and dedication might be such that the ensuing, unavoidable frictions would make life utterly miserable for both, and forced the apostle to mention in the following verses the possibility of divorce—the so-called Pauline Privilege:

"This is a great mystery, and I take it to mean Christ and the Church" (Eph. 5, 32)
St. Pauls tells us in Ephesians 5, 21–33, that marriage is a symbol of the union between Christ and the Church. Since the union between Christ and the Church can never be dissolved, so also marriage cannot be dissolved.

However, it must be asked again: To which kind of marriage did St. Paul refer? If one takes the present doctrine and practice of the Church as guide, it should apply solely to sacramental, consummated marriages. But this Paul could not have meant because he substantiates his teaching by reference to Genesis 2, 24 ("For this reason a man shall leave his father and mother and be joined to his wife, and the two shall become one"—Eph. 5, 31). It would be absurd to imply that in Genesis God should have spoken only of sacramental marriage, which then did not exist. And if the above text refers to marriage in general, or to all marriages, then the Church would be wrong in making use of such an authority in the Pauline Privilege and the Privilege of the Faith. This being inadmissible too, the answer is simply that St. Paul's words contain a beautiful symbol of marriage, but no legal norm concerning divorce.

" . . . She will be called an adulteress if she lives with another man while her husband is alive" (Rom. 7, 3)
St. Paul speaks here of a wife deserting her husband, which was legally unlawful by any existing law at that time. Nothing is said of the husband divorcing his wife, the normal case in the everyday circumstances of that period. This disparity can be explained by the prevailing legal inequality of the sexes. The apostle might have also wished to say something concerning the problem of remarriage of widows. The contents of Romans 7,

35

1–3, are matched by what is said in 1 Corinthians 7, 39–40. Even today it is often considered somewhat less than proper for a widow, but not a widower, to remarry; and frequently her disinclination to remarry might be regarded by her and others as a virtuous condition. Paul himself voiced the same opinion elsewhere, but here he had to affirm that with the death of the husband the marriage bond has come to a close.

7. THE DIFFERENCES BETWEEN GOSPEL TEXTS

Many proposals have been advanced to clarify the fact that Matthew should have the condition ("except for unchastity") while Mark and Luke have only the simple prohibition with no restrictive clause. One possible explanation would be that the Gospels reflect the teaching of Jesus according to the needs of the Christian community at the time of final composition of each of them.[1] Although the original, perhaps Aramaic, pre-Matthew is probably the oldest among the Gospel writings, the present Greek Matthew belongs probably to a later period than Mark and Luke. When the latter two Gospels received their final redaction, the life of the Christian community was in its inception and simpler. When the Greek Matthew was prepared for subsequent different and more sophisticated circumstances in which the problem of remarriage would have had to have been dealt with, the original *logion* of Jesus was remembered and preserved for posterity. The general principle of the sacredness and permanence of marriage as enunciated by Jesus was affirmed, but the exception to the rule, likewise established by him, was also mentioned.

---

1. Noonan has made the same observation. Speaking of various commands and counsels in the New Testament which have not been equalized in their binding force upon Christians, he says, "As neither an individual nor a society has ever existed which has taken all the texts of Scripture with equal literalness . . ." (*Contraception*, p. 37).

It could also be conjectured that Jesus in his reply referred solely to the Jewish toleration of divorce for reasons other than adultery of the wife. He affirmed the original ideal and divine purpose of marriage as permanent, and therefore also indissoluble, but as to the problem of an adulterous wife, he declined to decide anything concerning the husband's or wife's remarriage, and thus left it to the Church to develop and formulate the necessary doctrine in due time. This the Church did: the Eastern Churches permitted divorce and remarriage, the Western Church, at least since the beginning of the second millennium, forbade it.

8. EVANGELICAL COUNSEL, NOT LEGAL NORM

There is another possibility which ought to be considered, namely, that Jesus established a moral *ideal,* a counsel, without constituting it a legal norm. In connection with the Beatitudes he spoke also of divorce (Mt. 5, 27–32). One must therefore inquire if this is to be understood literally as a command or merely as a moral ideal. The subsequent verses treat of oaths, and Jesus expressly orders "do not swear at all." The Church, enlightened by the understanding of the Fathers, has understood this command as a moral ideal which does not bind in certain justified instances—and this in spite of the fact that there were and are Christian bodies which reject any kind of oath on the basis of the literal meaning of the passage.

Therefore, also, the foregoing prohibition of remarriage for the adulterous woman would be a legal norm only if tradition, and possibly the infallible teaching authority of the Church, understood it in this sense. As shall be seen in following chapters, there is sufficient evidence to indicate that the Christian antiquity did not regard the New Testament passages on divorce as legal norms which forbade any dissolution of marriage and remarriage.

37

9. THE INEQUALITY OF THE SEXES

It has been suggested that the principle forbidding remarriage to an adulterous wife applies also to the husband—although he is not mentioned—because of the equality of the sexes before the law of God. To us it seems that a distinction is to be made. While it is true that according to the teaching of Christianity the transgressions of man and woman are judged upon an equal footing as sins, this does not require that the legal consequences of human acts must be the same for both sexes.

Antiquity in general, and the Jewish world of the Old Testament not excluded, was androcentric, and was more concerned with the extramarital sins of wives, because of the greater peril to the structure of the family, than with those of the husband. Not only were the latter permitted to marry several wives, but sexual relationships with other women were not condemned. This is also the attitude of some modern legal systems, notably those which are based on the Code of Napoleon. The reason for the different treatment is to be found in the allegedly greater exposure of the man to temptations of such kind, to the different upbringing of the sexes in our civilization, and to the inequality of the sexes in respect to the norms of behavior in probably all human societies. It might be politically prudent, therefore, to formulate the legal consequences of illicit sexual behavior in conformity with these differences, and to treat the sexual transgressions of husbands more leniently than those of wives.

Inequality of the sexes in the realm of law can be deduced also from the permission granted by Jesus that the husband could dismiss an adulterous wife by a writ of divorce. This was a continuance of the Jewish law. However, there was no such thing as a writ of divorce that a wife could issue; only a husband possessed this right. If Jesus permitted the writ of divorce in a specific instance, he also permitted the difference in legal treatment of the sexes.

10. CONCLUSION

To the question whether holy Scripture will lose its value as a book of commandments and rules of life in respect to the institution of Christian matrimony one must reply, certainly not. One should, however, be aware that the Bible is not a textbook of natural history, biology, or human history, nor is it a code of canon law. The Western mentality has always preferred to look towards the negative side, to where the exact limitations are clearly defined, and beyond which lie sin. The Christian East has sought rather to set up goals towards which man is urged to strive, each according to his own spiritual insight, and without his being held accountable if he is sincerely unable to reach some higher goal because of human weakness. In respect to the durability of individual marriages, the Christian East is dedicated to the same ideal, namely, that it was Christ's wish and counsel that marriage ought to be dissolved by death alone, and that the spouses should forgive all of each other's trespasses, including adultery. However, as provided by the Old Testament as well as by all ancient civilizations, the Eastern Churches have understood always that Jesus did not prohibit total divorce and remarriage.

II.

DIVORCE IN THE HISTORY OF THE CHURCH

1. THE USE OF HISTORICAL EVIDENCE

BEFORE embarking on a study of the problem of divorce in various eras of Church history, it will be necessary to make some general observations on the way Catholic theologians have tried to find support for the absolute prohibition of divorce in history.

In judging the historical value of a certain witness in tradition, only scientific criteria are to be applied. One cannot consider some as more important, and assign to them first rank, solely because they help uphold a certain teaching. Not a few authors, in the study of historical evidence for or against divorce, divide the Fathers, writers, or synods into two categories: the correct ones are those who exclude divorce, and the erroneous ones those who permit it.

However, a dogmatic proposition such as that of the absolute indissolubility of sacramental marriage, is right or wrong because of the truth it contains, not because of the existence or absence of historical proofs. But if one wishes to find out whether ecclesiastical tradition supported or rejected a given teaching, it is necessary to approach the search without preconceived notions, and without antecedent value judgments. The only criterion can be the prominence of the author as a historic person: his learning, his orthodoxy in other areas of sacred science, his capability to make distinctions and write calmly without personal, political, racial, etc., bias. In addition, whatever remains unclear in his expressions is to be interpreted in the light of his times, and cannot be corrected by the importation of present-day ideas.

Any other method of investigation, especially if it is used in the furthering of theological understanding, cannot be called research; actually, it is no inquiry at all because the answer is already contained in the question. Catholic doctrine, if so infallibly established by the Church, is true whether or not historical witnesses should be in disagreement with it. But to gather evidence for the truth of a Catholic tenet, or what is regarded at that time to be the doctrine of the Church, by interpreting the meaning of facts in the light of preconceived—even if dogmatically true—propositions is not scientific research, and merely lends support to the conviction of the secular learned professions that theology, especially Catholic theology, does not belong to the body of scientific human knowledge.[1]

It cannot be denied that there are passages found in the writings of the Fathers which express opposition to divorce without clearly defining a position on remarriage. However, speaking speculatively, one must assume that the Fathers and ancient synods could have had before their minds several situations, each quite different from the other in its legal significance: (1) They could have completely excluded any divorce whatsoever. (2) They could have disapproved of divorce as a morally regrettable happening, and have expressed their opinion in severe words of condemnation, without the intention of excluding it as a legal institution. (3) They could have prohibited divorce effected by private decision, whether according to the Jewish example by the husband alone, or by mutual agreement of the spouses. (4) They could have con-

---

1. While later theologians, such as Rokosvany and Perrone in the 19th century, liberally imply that those who might be wrong in admitting the existence of absolute divorce in the early Church are also necessarily morally evil, previous centuries did not hesitate to use such devices as deleting parts of historical testimony attesting to the permissibility of divorce. For example, St. Ivo of Chartres quoted in his collection of laws canons of the Council of Verberie, but omitted all passages referring to the permission of remarriage granted to divorced husbands (see I. Fahrner, *Geschichte des Unauflöslichkeitsprinzips und der vollkommenen Scheidung der Ehe im kanonischen Recht*, p. 115).

demned those divorces which were granted without reasons justifying them. (5) They could have voiced disapproval of divorce based on the unjust desertion of the spouse. (6) They could have recommended as a counsel or ideal that spouses remain unmarried after separation, without excluding the right of divorce, although this advice might have been expressed in words which made it appear to be an injunction. For it is patent that not all theologians have the talent to express themselves as would a legislator. (7) Their words could have meant practical acceptance of the inequality of the sexes before the law; in other words, while the adultery of the man was no less sinful than that of the woman, the juridical consequences could be unequal, and thus might permit divorce in the case of an adulterous wife and deny it because of adultery committed by the husband.

In studying the meaning of passages of the Fathers referring to divorce, these and additional possibilities must be considered if one wishes to arrive at a valid interpretation.

The fact that divorce was rare in the West before the beginning of the second millennium, or not a frequent occurrence as it is today, need not be explained as due to the opposition of the Church, where and when such opposition in fact existed. It can be also accounted for by social custom, in a culture where the elders decided who would marry whom, on what conditions, and whether the marriage contract, sanctioned by tangible pecuniary stipulations, could be rescinded. Divorce will be rare in such a hieratic society, and the problem will not be discussed much by contemporary authors; nor would ecclesiastical legislators be expected to take cognizance of a relatively minor problem. Thus from the absence of express permissions of divorce, which could have been preserved in the writings of Fathers and legislative activity of synods, nothing can be concluded.

It is true that the Western Church never sanctioned divorce in a synod as important as that of Trullo (692) in the Byzantine Church, but merely by decrees of smaller synods. However, this can be easily explained, since there simply was no general synod of the Western Church before I Lateran (1123). The earlier dogmatic synods of the West, for example that of Orange (529), were not convoked nor did they issue their decisions as ecumenical but rather as reflecting the opinion of a particular Church. Their dogmatic decrees became universal because other Churches accepted them, especially when they received the approval of the Roman See.

The absence of general decrees in the Western Church sanctioning complete separation and remarriage is, therefore, no testimony to their prohibition; it is not an *argumentum e silentio,* for nobody spoke of it *at all.*

A certain proof from silence does, however, seem permissible. From the absence of historical evidence that would show how the ancient Church tried to enforce the indissolubility of sacramental marriage against the permissive attitude of the secular power, the valid conclusion can be drawn that the Church did not regard divorce as absolutely prohibited. All tendencies leading towards a weakening of the bond of marriage were naturally deplored and condemned, and the scandalous example of emperors and other public figures was publicly and privately censured by bishops and ecclesiastical writers. The vocabulary used for decrying the evil of breaking up marriages and contracting others might be passionate, and the new unions might be called adulterous; but all this does not necessarily prove that total divorce was judged legally impossible. One can therefore realize how mistaken are, for example, Wernz, Vidal, and Aguirre, authors of the canonical work *Ius Canonicum ad Codicis Normam Exactum,* when they state that "the Church was unable easily to obtain in the Roman Empire, especially the Eastern, an accurate and universal observance of the law of the Gospel." [2] Rather, the absence of a concerted and systematic fight by the Eastern Church against the imperial legislation permitting divorce ought to be inter-

2. P. 787.

preted as reflecting the mind of the Church—different from that of the Catholic Church today—that divorce was not prohibited by the law of Jesus.

After a study of the testimony of tradition given in the following sections and of the pertinent texts in the appendixes, the reader will understand why one can consider as exaggerations such statements as, for example, "The Catholic Church and Catholic theology have always maintained . . ." or "The testimonies of the Fathers and of the councils leave us no room for doubt that . . ." [3] This is simply not true. There are only a few documents before the end of the first millennium attesting to the absolute rejection of divorce. Only after the reform of Cluny in the tenth century and the foundation of the first universities can it be said that the Western Church established a clear policy and doctrine prohibiting divorce; and the fact is that there is no document of the first centuries which would clearly and unequivocally exclude divorce in the case of adultery on the part of the wife and at the same time forbid a subsequent remarriage of the innocent husband. Or to say it more plainly: there are no witnesses of the early Church—as long as we do not lose sight of the necessary distinction among related legal concepts—which would support the present Catholic doctrine on the indissolubility of sacramental marriages.

For the present purpose it would be sufficient to submit testimony by a not too small number of witnesses to the effect that divorce and remarriage were permitted in not too rare instances. This would establish the absence of a uniform, determined doctrine on this subject. But actually the passages gathered from the writings of various authors and the canons of synods, patriarchs, and popes, insinuating the permissibility of divorce are so numerous that there cannot be any doubt of the absence of the principle of absolute indissolubility.

3. See for example A. Piolanti: "An apodictic proof is offered by the words of Christ . . ."; ". . . the limpid affirmation of the Council of Trent" (*I Sacramenti*, p. 671).

44

Divorce and remarriage were permitted only to the husband and solely for adultery committed by his wife. This was justified by Matthew 19, 9. For a long time there was no remedy for an innocent wife abandoned unjustly by her husband. Only in later centuries did some authorities permit her a remarriage after a certain waiting period.

Thus when one leafs through the pages of statements on the problem of divorce in the ancient world, one nearly always reads solely of the problem of remarriage of a divorced wife. It was clear that an adulterous wife did not deserve any consideration, but when it was the case of an innocent woman, it was not easy for the Church to forbid her remarriage. The scarcity of references to husbands is to be understood in the light of the legal inequality of the spouses. It had been accepted by the Church that husbands could separate themselves from an adulterous wife and remarry, and there was no need for discussion of this matter. Catholic theologians who wish to interpret the prohibitions found in contemporary documents against wives remarrying after being abandoned by their husbands are at a loss because it is obvious that the extramarital affairs of husbands must have been a much more frequent occurrence than those of the wives. Why is the husband's case mentioned so rarely? The answer is that a husband could divorce and remarry according to the practice of the Church, while the remarriage of the wife was as a rule excluded.

Some Catholic authors attempt to explain the permission of divorce attested to by a number of documents as referring to a simple separation from bed, board, and dwelling. This they do because they are ignorant of the fact that no civil law of ancient time knew of such separation. Neither the Jewish law nor that of the Roman Empire envisioned in the termination of marital unions anything less than total divorce. How could a wife separate herself from her husband without having the support of civil law in enforcing alimony? If she was prevented from remarriage because she was still bound to him, how could she provide for herself in an economy in which women had no opportunity of gainful employment outside the precincts of the home? Since there was no such legal institution as separation, it cannot be that the Church authorities recommended it, and it must be assumed that the Fathers did not refer to it; when they permitted divorce of a marriage, it meant total dissolution of the bond with permission to remarriage.

Even when in the writings of the Fathers divorce is condemned and associated with the sin of adultery, it does not necessarily follow that they considered new marriages entered by divorced Christians as canonically invalid. On the contrary, there is testimony to the effect that after such members of the Church had done penance under the supervision of the bishop for several years they could be readmitted to communion with their second spouses. This concept of penance, performed publicly under the scrutiny of the Church, included the idea that it was not only an atonement for past transgressions, but that it could also rectify illicit legal situations which had had their beginning in the sinful act. Thus men and women who remarried after they had unjustifiably abandoned spouses or had been repudiated because of adultery were subjected to public penance for a number of years with a view afterwards to being admitted to communion. In other words, their second marital union ultimately received recognition.

This idea of penance is still evident in the practice of the Roman Curia when religious, especially those with solemn profession of perpetual vows, receive a dispensation and are permitted to return to the world. Not rarely a lifelong penance is imposed upon them such as the weekly recitation of certain prayers. Similarly, the Russian orthodox Church permitted a third marriage only on condition that a penance (*epitimia*) be accepted by the beneficiary.[4]

One can make the general statement that the Fathers were

4. See *Appendix*, St. Basil (cans. 9, 77); Egbert of York; Alexius Studites; Milevis (can. 17); Verberie (can. 9); *Penitential of Theodore*. See also F. Heiler, *Urkirche und Ostkirche*, p. 280.

primarily interested in rectifying hardship caused to the individual and not with upholding the common good independently of the good of the individual. They considered the purpose of the salvific mission of the Son of God to be directed to the good of the persons. Of course, public order also had to be maintained because the interests of individuals are tied to its orderly conservation. However, when there is a conflict between the welfare of the individual and the preservation of the common good, dispensations may be granted. In reading the relevant passages of the Fathers one becomes aware of their hesitation in lending support to what might be regarded as an infraction of established principles; but then, in accordance with the yet undeveloped doctrine, the Fathers yield to their sense of mercy, to what they call Christian "condescension." They profess to do this as spokesmen of the Church, who as the bride of Christ possesses the necessary authority for the adjustment of the law to the needs of individuals.

It is true that there were clashes between the Church and civil law, even after the Roman Empire had outlawed paganism and given to Christianity the status of an established Church. Complete harmony was never achieved; but neither can every relaxation of church law necessarily be traced back to the influence of civil law and interpreted as the subjection of the Church to the secular power. Western Catholic theologians have tried to explain the permission of divorce and remarriage, as documented in the Roman Empire and especially in the Near East, as a surrender by the Church of the doctrinal principles of indissolubility to civil authority.

It cannot be denied that the Church mitigated her attitude towards second and further marriages of the faithful and thereby met the civil law half way. But this has the significance of a temporal coincidence, and it is not necessary to see a causal relationship. The Church was guided by the principle of Jesus as announced in Matthew 19, 9, namely, that there was a ground for divorce, adultery. The Eastern Churches interpreted

47

this as referring not only to the actual sin, but also to those circumstances in which the estrangement of the spouses had progressed to such a degree that adultery could be considered virtually an accomplished fact even if not yet executed.

The marriage law of the Church continued to be developed during the centuries of the great migrations of the Germanic and Slavic peoples into Europe. The evolution is to be viewed as a consequent unfolding of fundamental principles and their application to new situations. Remarriage was thus permitted to a wife who had been abandoned by her husband, without his charging her with adultery. We even find instances when mutal consent could be a divorce ground. Similarly, when there occurred raids by Vikings, Saracens, and other barbarian tribes into Western Europe—which had as aim the abduction of prisoners who were made slaves—the separated spouses were permitted to remarry after a certain period of waiting, although the first marriage was sometimes reestablished when the kidnapped spouses were able to return. Also, entrance into the religious life, with the consent of the spouse, dissolved a marriage and permitted the other spouse to remarry—as also was the practice in the Eastern Churches.

One can assert, speaking only quantitatively, that is, looking at the amount of documents from those times, and not so much to the qualitative value of each, that up to the eleventh century there was no difference between the Eastern and Western Churches in the question of divorce. It was permitted for many grounds, although isolated voices were heard which sought to allow divorce on the basis of adultery alone. These few representatives of a stricter interpretation of the law on divorce gained a larger audience during the Gregorian reform, so that in the Western Church of the twelfth century it came to be accepted, at least theoretically, that all divorces of sacramental marriages are forbidden. The tradition of the ancient Church and the practice of the Eastern Churches was ignored, partially because of the now accomplished schism, and partially because of the lack of easily accessible patristic documents.

2. THE HISTORICAL OVERVIEW

A historian, not influenced by any preconceived notions, who follows the path of the legal institution of divorce, or its opposite, the prohibition of divorce, through the centuries of Church history, will find that in the East there is an uninterrupted evolvement of the idea that marriages ought to be permitted to be dissolved and that at least innocent partners be allowed to contract new marriages. In the West he will encounter a different development.

The institution of marriage was ordained by God to be a permanent, enduring association between a man and a woman, and ideally it should last till the death of one spouse dissolves it. However, permanency and indissolubility are not to be confused. It is also true, of course, that the Gospels relate the teaching of Jesus in such a way that divorce is considered only as an extreme measure, while there is no *express* mention of a possible second marriage for a divorced partner.

This rule was broken the first time by St. Paul himself when he found it necessary to permit divorce and remarriage to those Christians who found themselves married to spouses who did not accept Christianity and thus made life difficult according to the exacting expectations of the early Church. The apostle was quite conscious that he had no support in the tradition of Jesus' teaching (1 Cor. 7, 12) as it was known to him from oral information, since at the time of the writing of his letters the four Gospels had not been formulated in writing. It was also assumed by him, and probably confirmed in the experience of everyday life, that a marriage of two Christians would ordinarily not so deteriorate as to create a need for divorce, but should it happen, the wife must remain single (1 Tim. 5, 3; 1 Cor. 7, 11). Nothing was said as to whether the husband could remarry, but only that he should not divorce his wife.

Turning now to the post-apostolic time, it must be admitted that in the writings from the first three centuries there are few references to divorce. The reasons for this paucity of mate-

49

rial mentioning divorce are many: persecution from the state led to higher standards of selection of prospective members of the Church; while the number of Christians married to infidel spouses was great, there existed the expedient of the Pauline Privilege; to this group belonged also numerous converts who postponed baptism to the later part of their lives, and received this sacrament of initiation only at the end; the social setting of small, tightly knit groups was conducive to the stability of marriages; the expectation of a second coming of Christ discouraged the idea of second marriages; absolute monogamy was counseled by Paul himself (1 Cor. 7, 8); virginity received a special status in the Church, while a negative attitude towards sexuality prevailed for centuries;[1] heretical teachings concerning marriage, such as those of the Montanists, Manichaeans, Encratides, and various Gnostic factions forced the Church into a pattern of rigidity rather than of relaxation with regard to marital discipline. However, while the first centuries yield only few references favorable to divorce, neither do they furnish testimony for its absolute exclusion. It is therefore also to be expected that a condemnation of divorce as a moral evil would be sometimes displayed, although there was no doctrinal principle formed as to its legal implications (Hermas, Clement of Alexandria, Ambrose of Milan). Whenever we encounter a prohibition of remarriage after divorce, it first is directed to wives, while there is no mention of the husbands and their legal situation, or second, divorce is declared permissible solely because of adultery, or third, divorce is disapproved for specific causes other then adultery (Justin Martyr, Origen, Cyprian, Hilary of Poitiers, Gregory of Nazianzus, Chromatius of Aquileia, John Chrysostom, Jerome, Theodoret of Cyprus; also the Apostolic Canons, the synods of Elvira [300] and Angers [453]; Innocent I, Leo I, Gregory I).

With the gaining of freedom, legal recognition, and finally also the institutionalization of the Church after Constantine, the social setting changed, and the problem of divorce-remarriage

1. See E. Schillebeeckx, *Marriage. Human Reality and Saving Mystery,* p. 148, and Noonan, *Contraception,* pp. 70–79.

was more frequently mentioned in the writings of those centuries. Marriage was still something outside the direct control of the Church. Although recognized as a sacred institution, the marital bond was governed by civil legislation. Their expressions are not always unambiguous, but one can say that the institution of divorce as such was not rejected by the Fathers, and that they sought to oppose only certain features, as, for example, divorce by mutual agreement of the spouses, and the writ of divorce given by a wife to her husband. The right of the husband to divorce an adulterous wife was always upheld, and he was considered justified in marrying another woman (Origen, Lactantius, Basil the Great, Ambrosiaster, Asterius of Amasea, Epiphanius of Salamis, Victor of Antioch, Avitus of Vienna; Arles [314], Milevis [416], Vannes [461], Agde [506]).

No attempt was made by the early Church to establish marriage tribunals. The subjection of Christians to the Roman judiciary was accepted as a normal fact of life, and marriage cases were brought before civil law courts. From this followed also a global acknowledgment of civil marriage law, including the possibility of divorce—although some Fathers objected to the civil law, which punished infractions on the part of the wife while allowing unlimited sexual liberty to the husband (John Chrysostom, Jerome, Augustine).

This general acceptance of civil law explains why we cannot expect, and actually do not encounter, explicit and unequivocal rejection of divorce. It was simply not necessary for the writers to mention what was known to everybody as allowed, namely, the remarriage of innocent husbands. But it did have to be inculcated again and again that the wife was not legally entitled to the same rights according to the law of God as interpreted by the Church. Since this latter teaching was opposed to the law of the state, it had to be spelled out by the Fathers again and again.

But gradually these limitations too were relaxed: as we have seen, consensual divorce, with the right of remarriage, was accepted if the other spouse entered religious life. Some Fathers felt obliged to permit innocent wives, maliciously deserted by their husbands, to remarry. These and other relaxations were granted by the Fathers in the belief that such mercy or condescension (Origen, Basil the Great) behooved the Church.

With the progressive disintegration of the Roman Empire in the West and the influx of the Germanic peoples into Europe new social problems arose. Augustine of Hippo developed from various passages of the New Testament that doctrine on marriage in general and on dissolubility in particular which today is the official teaching of the Catholic Church. But for a time his opinions remained largely disregarded. The renaissance of Western ecclesiastical law in the newly organized Germanic states in France, Germany, northern Italy, Spain, led to a voluminous conciliar legislation. In addition to the divorce grounds previously mentioned, voluntary and involuntary desertion was added (Theodore of Canterbury, Venerable Bede, Boniface of Mainz, Egbert of York, Megingoz, Nicephorus of Constantinople, Gregory II, Zachary, Stephen II, Stephen III, Eugene II, Leo IV; Orleans [533], Hereford [673], Hibernia Secunda [7th c.], Soissons [744], Verberie [752], Compiegne [757], and also completely unlimited consensual divorces were recognized [Formularies of Marculf and of Angers]).[2]

The Carolingian reform initiated a counter-movement. The theology of Augustine was again propagated (Friuli [791], Paris [829], Nantes [875], Tribur [895], Ingelheim [948]), although the application of the new principles was successfully resisted for several centuries, as is evident in subsequent canonical collections (Regino of Prüm, Burchard of Worms). The absolute indissolubility of marriage was promoted by the Cluniac reform, and the doctrine became generally accepted in the West in the wake of the Gregorian reform (11th c.). The

2. It is not true that this was a consequence of subservience of the Frankish Church to the state, as is proved by such instances as the opposition of bishop Germanus of Paris to the marriage of King Charibert to a blood relation: the king was finally excommunicated (see D. S. Bailey, *Sexual Relation in Christian Thought*, p. 108).

newly founded universities gave the Augustinian view a systematic and scholastic foundation, and the Decree of Gratian established it firmly throughout the Western Church.

The end of the first millennium witnessed a disintegration of the Germanic states. The emperors and kings were engaged in a battle with the lesser chiefs who challenged their supremacy. The monarchs found in the hierarchy of the Church capable allies in this struggle with the rising aristocracy and they soon made the bishops and abbots territorial vassals of the crown, because the law of celibacy prevented them from beginning hereditary lines of succession. While previously matrimonial legislation was exercised either by the organs of the state alone or in mixed assemblies of the barons and the hierarchy, now this jurisdiction shifted to the ecclesiastics. The feudal system empowered the bishops and abbots, as the only vassals capable of organizing the ecclesiastical as well as the secular sphere, to legislate and administer both. The Western doctrine of the Church therefore triumphed over the more traditional civil allowance of dissolubility of marriages. The reaction to this new legal code was not as pronounced as one would expect, probably because there still existed the expedient of annulments of marriages—which was liberally exercised for several centuries. Even after Trent (1565) the decision of one diocesan tribunal was sufficient to establish invalidity and permit a new marriage; and only with Benedict XIV (Constitution *Dei Miseratione,* 1741) did the defender of the bond become obliged to appeal from the sentence of the first tribunal to a higher court.[3]

Later centuries saw a partial breakdown of the principle of absolute indissolubility: the Pauline Privilege was more freely applied and the dispensative dissolution of non-consummated sacramental marriages was evolved. Since the beginning of expanded missionary efforts among pagan peoples, the Privilege of the Faith (Petrine Privilege) was elaborated and also defined as broadly as possible.

3. W. M. Plöchl, *Geschichte des Kirchenrechts,* vol. IV, pp. 399f.

At the Council of Trent there was a group of bishops who wished to see defined against the Protestant teaching that marriage pertained to the state and that divorce can be permitted, the absolute and perpetual indissolubility of Christian marriage. However, for reasons described in another chapter, this aim was not achieved, and the doctrine as accepted today in the Catholic Church is only a *propositio fidei proxima*. Today all kinds of marriages are considered to be dissoluble, and they are actually readily dissolved either by direct (papal dispensation) or indirect (dispensation from interpellations) intervention of ecclesiastical authorities, with the exception of one kind: the consummated, sacramental marriage, that is, that class which affects the largest group of Catholics.

During all these centuries, all the Eastern Churches, anti-Chalcedonian no less than the Orthodox, permitted and permit divorce and remarriage in respect to all marriages.

3. THE WITNESS OF THE FATHERS

The seeming daring assertion made in this book that the passages referring to divorce and remarriage found in the writings of the Fathers have generally been incorrectly explained, must be and can be substantiated only by quoting the respective texts. It would have been insufficient merely to have given a brief summary of the information with references to the patristic collection in which they can be located. For the evidence derived from the Fathers is not so much of a direct and positive nature as it is an argument from silence; that is, the absence of explicit prohibition of divorce-remarriage with regard to either spouse or at least with regard to the husband where such a verdict could rightfully be expected.

It is also not possible to assert that specific trends can be found among the Fathers in respect to the admissibility of divorce-remarriage, and then to group the passages according to these trends; the material is so varied that it was judged more expedient to list them in approximate chronological order.

Also, it was thought inadvisable to divide the patristic testimony into Eastern and Western because in the period of history we are concerned with the separation of the two cultures did not as yet influence theological opinion—at least not in this area. However, it is not maintained that the writings of the Fathers exhibit a clear tendency towards the approval of the remarriage of divorced Christians, but solely that there are no indications in the documents which would permit one to conclude that they consistently opposed it in principle.

In offering passages in Appendix I from ecclesiastical writers of the first millennium of Christianity, those which referred to the dissolution of natural, non-sacramental marriages have been omitted since they do not relate to the present problem of sacramental marriages. Also, witnesses from the Eastern Churches after the sixth century were generally not included since at that time it was everywhere in the East recognized that the Church can and actually does grant the dissolution of sacramental marriages, at least in cases of adultery.

Admittedly, this detailing of texts will give the impression of repetitiousness. However, this fact is just the cardinal point. It is correct, as a number of theologians have had to concede, that some Fathers and synods give reserved approval to divorce-remarriage; yet what is even more significant is that only very few Fathers exclude it explicitly. This absence of utterances which one would expect can be demonstrated only by listing as many passages as feasible.

4. THE WITNESS OF THE ROMAN PONTIFFS

We have examined the pronouncements of popes separately in an appendix because it is assumed that they were more aware of the import their decisions or declarations, even if *obiter dicta,* would have for the Church. This gives them also a higher probative value in either direction, as approving or disapproving divorce.

The scarcity of papal utterances on the subject of total divorce is certainly not without significance. After all, civil law and the custom of the Churches permitted it, at least in respect to the innocent husband, and if this was considered against the law of God, we would expect more protestations than actually have been discovered.

In order to explain or justify those documents of popes or synods which clearly concede the remarriage of divorced Christians, much has been made of the assumed need of the Church to tolerate an abuse that she could not prevent, and of her timidity before the secular power. However, we have so many examples of courageous popes protesting against encroachments of the Byzantine emperors that the assumption of lack of courage or fear of possible repercussions on the part of the Roman pontiffs cannot explain sufficiently the absence of remonstrances.

The great student of Eastern marriage law, Joseph Zhishman, underlines the readiness of the Church to speak out against those laws of the Byzantine state which were regarded as opposing fundamental religious concepts of marriage according to Eastern understanding—as, for example, when some emperors attempted to contract a fourth marriage—although the protests were followed, as expected, by brutal persecution and martyrdom. On the other hand, there is the absence of any protest on the part of the popes, patriarchs, and bishops against the civil legislation of the Byzantine emperors permitting divorce. This fact cannot be explained by lack of information, concern, or moral courage, but finds its most natural answer in the assumption that the hierarchy did not consider it inconsistent with the teaching or the practice of the Church. No protest of Pope Vigilius is recorded against the 117th Novella of Justinian (541), or of other popes or patriarchs against the legislation establishing legal conditions for divorce and remarriage issued by Basil the Macedonian, Leo the Philosopher, or Constantine VII Porphyrogenetos between 807 and 959.[1]

1. *Das Eherecht der orientalischen Kirche,* pp. 114f.

Many Catholic authors cannot avoid admitting that the Christian East always permitted divorce and remarriage, but they wish to enhance the reputation of the Western Church by affirming that the Roman Church always opposed divorce and remarriage. However, the question arises whether this assertion is in conformity with the historical truth.

A. Freisen, whose monumental *Geschichte des katholischen Eherechts bis zum Verfall der Glossenliteratur* (History of Catholic Marriage Law up to the Decline of the Glossators) is still considered so valuable that a reprint of the second edition of 1893 was put on the market as recently as 1963, has a special chapter on divorce and the oldest beliefs of the Roman Church in this matter.[2] Of the eight pages of text only one is devoted to the Roman witnesses on this problem, namely, Hermas, Innocent I, and Gregory I. While it is true that for this period no Roman witness is extant that would expressly permit remarriage after divorce, and we admit that divorce with or without remarriage was certainly morally disapproved, it cannot be said, on the basis of the lack of documentation, that there existed a well-established Roman conviction excluding it. Since the doctrine of absolute indissolubility of Christian marriage was not yet—and still is not according to our opinion—an infallible teaching of the Church, no doctrinal or disciplinary inferrence can be drawn from this dearth of papal pronouncements.

5. THE WITNESS OF THE SYNODS

Synods of the First Millennium

The testimony of the Church is especially expressed by the enactments of the legislative assemblies of her hierarchy, the bishops, gathered in various local synods and councils. Gen-

2. Pp. 769–776.

erally speaking, we can expect that the bishops will deal with such matters of practical importance that are not yet sufficiently defined in the law of the Church. What the clergy and faithful consider securely established in law, is not questioned in everyday life, even if it is not observed, and bishops do not feel compelled to enact laws for unquestioned problems.

As will be shown in the documents quoted in Appendix III, divorce and remarriage were regarded as permissible for a husband, and solely for him, because of adultery of the wife, and reference was made to Matthew 19, 9. This was therefore not defined anew in the canons of the synods. What had to be proscribed and condemned were attempts by husbands to repudiate wives for reasons other than adultery and then to contract new marriages. Another problem was that of private divorces, especially when the husband expelled his wife, which denied the official Church the opportunity to assure herself that the Gospel prescriptions had not been trespassed. Another question not easily settled was the situation of an innocent wife, deserted by her husband, and a possible second marriage for her.

The larger number of the documents quoted in Appendix III refer to the Church in Gaul; councils of the Eastern Churches are not considered here, since they evidently permitted divorce and remarriage by common law, and had no need to speak of this topic. From the prevalence of documents from the time of the Merovingians and Carolingians, Catholic authors draw the conclusion that this is a sign of decadent laxism, and of the special proclivities of the Germanic tribes, especially of the Franks. To this it can be said that some of the councils go back to the time before the coming of the Germanic nations into Gaul. Also the absence of corresponding legislative efforts in other parts of the Western Church of those times does not prove that elsewhere divorce and remarriage were unknown, but rather that the misfortunes of political upheavals, of unceasing warfare against marauding tribes in Italy, the religious disturbances caused by the Arian

Goths in the Iberian Peninsula and by the Vandals in Northern Africa, the tumultuous settlement of South Eastern Europe by the Slavs—all explain sufficiently why we have such a preponderance of documents allowing divorce and remarriage from the Church in Gaul. If we were to summarize the legal situation on this question between the years 400 and 900 in the Eastern and Western Church, we could say that the marriage bond was dissoluble nearly everywhere on the ground of adultery committed by the wife, and when one of the spouses chose religious life. Should there be found a few voices opposing it, they are rather the lone exceptions, abstracting now from the question whether they were right or wrong. Even if the contents of such documents exclude the permissibility of divorce, their language is never clear to such a degree as to be an unequivocal affirmation of the present-day teaching of Catholic theologians.

Both because special importance is to be attached to the work of such synods which had the character of ecumenical councils, as those of Lyons (1274), Ferrara-Florence (1438), and Trent (1545–1565), and because they bring us into the modern era of the Church, we shall now examine their proceedings.

Lyons and Ferrara-Florence

The two union councils of Lyons and Ferrara-Florence did not take a position on divorce as one would expect if the present Catholic doctrine had been considered completely established at that time. This would seem to be a valid *argumentum e silentio*. But an example of how this argument can be reversed is to be found in a work by G. Perrone, one of the great Catholic dogmaticians of the nineteenth century.[1] Since the Greeks in their accusations of the Catholic Church never mentioned the

---

1. *De Matrimonio Christiano*, vol. III, p. 393.

denial of divorce as one of the heresies or errors of the Western Church, including here Photius and Caerularius, Perrone draws the conclusion that the Greek Church considered the position of the Roman Church correct and unassailable. The facts were just the reverse. As one can glean from the study of so many documents of the Fathers, councils, and popes, the Eastern as well as the Western Church granted divorce up to the time of Cerularius within approximately the same limits. Even the unfriendliest Greek was unaware of any difference in this matter between the Churches, and saw no reason to mention or oppose anything. One can turn the argument around and ask why the Western Church did not during these centuries accuse the Greek or the Eastern Churches of heresy in granting divorce and permission of remarriage.

The Second Ecumenical Council of Lyons was held by Pope Gregory X in 1274 and had as its main purpose the reunion of the Greek with the Western Church. Emperor Michael Palaelogus submitted a statement in the form of a letter addressed to the Pope who accepted it. It is a description of what the Emperor regarded as the faith of the Roman Church. Implicitly, he declared his own belief in it. But by no means can this letter be considered a document of the Council, much less a dogmatic or doctrinal decision.

Concerning the sacrament of matrimony the Emperor says, "But in respect to marriage [the Roman Church] holds that neither is a man permitted to have several wives, nor a woman to have several men. After a legitimate marriage had been dissolved by the death of one of the spouses, she says that second and third marriages thereafter in succession are permitted, except if a canonical impediment stands against it." [2]

2. "De matrimonio vero tenet (romana ecclesia) quod nec unus vir plures uxores simul, nec una mulier permittitur habere plures viros. Soluto vero legitimo matrimonio per mortem coniugum alterius, secundas et tertias deinde nuptias successive licitas esse dicit, si impedimentum canonicum aliud ex causa aliquid non obsistat" (*Sacrorum Conciliorum Nova et Amplissima Collectio*, ed. Mansi, vol. XXIV, col. 71).

From these words the following conclusions can be drawn: (1) Simultaneous polygamy, either polygyny or polyandry, is forbidden. (2) Successive marriages are permitted, and the practice of the Greek Church to permit a third marriage only in exceptional circumstances is thereby rejected. However, it is significant that no reference was made to a fourth and further marriage, which the Greeks considered forbidden by divine law, but which the Latin Church permitted freely. (3) The Roman Church was convinced that marriage is dissolved by death alone, because otherwise specific mention of divorce would have been made. (4) No allusion to or condemnation of the Greek practice of granting divorce because of adultery was attempted, nor was it included in the list of Greek errors circulated in connection with the Council. Since it was known in the Western Church that the Greek Church granted divorces and permitted remarriage during the lifetime of the other spouse, the silence of Western theologians and Fathers at the Council can be explained only if one assumes that they were not totally convinced that it was a necessary doctrine of the Church. Otherwise, they would have felt obliged to remonstrate as they did with regard to the Greek depreciation of a third marriage.

For the Council of Florence one knows that no decision was taken in this respect, and actually no official discussion took place on the question of divorce. The Greeks were in an official way questioned on this point in the presence of Pope Eugene IV. They replied that this was in conformity with the Gospel and the teaching of the Eastern Fathers. No further talks were held on this subject, and although the Pope and the Latin Council members most certainly disagreed in theory and practice, the difference was not judged an obstacle to reunion.

It is true that the so-called *Decretum pro Armenis* (*Exultate Deo*) of Eugene IV, issued November 22, 1438, contains a mention of the doctrine of indissolubility: "Although it is permitted to separate matrimonial cohabitation because of fornication, it is nevertheless not allowed to contract another marriage, because the bond of marriage which was lawfully contracted is perpetual." [3]

This decree was by many theologians (Vasquez, Suarez, Billot) considered a dogmatic definition, but other students deny this (d'Annibale, Pietro Gasparri, Van Rossum). But it cannot be considered either an infallible decision or a true conciliar document; it was nothing else than an authoritative instruction governing pastoral practice.[4] If it had been a dogmatic definition, a new attempt at another definition at the Council of Trent would have been regarded as superfluous. Although it is included into the acts of the Council of Florence, one can hardly compare the submission of two representatives of the Armenian Church, who signed what was laid before them, with the reunion effected by the entire Western Church and the Byzantine emperor and the numerous representatives of the Greek hierarchy in Florence after prolonged and profound discussions.

Trent

It is the general conviction of Catholics, including the hierarchy and clergy, that the question of a possible divorce of sacramental, consummated marriages has been authoritatively settled by the decision of the Council of Trent.

3. "Quamvis ex causa fornicationis liceat tori separationem facere, non tamen aliud matrimonium contrahere fas est, cum matrimonii vinculum legitime contractum perpetuum sit."
4. The same decree is said to be positively erroneous in its definition of the matter of the sacrament of holy orders as the "transmission of the instruments" (altar missal, paten, chalice, etc.). On this subject, Noldin-Schmitt-Heinzel say, "Although such doctrinal decrees are not absolutely infallible, they nevertheless surpass by far the authority of a private man . . . It is thus not enough to give them mere external assent, that is, by not speaking or writing against them, but all Christians are obliged to hold them true by internal assent, until the contrary is proved with certainty . . . just as Cardinal Van Rossum did not hesi-

It is true that there is a definition of the Council of Trent on this matter, but, as we will see, it does not declare what is generally assumed to be its meaning. In order to understand the work of the Council, it is necessary to know the reasons for its convocation, and to be acquainted with the problematic with which the Council had to wrestle.

One of the ideas current at the time of the Protestant Reformation separated in marriage the sacrament from the contract. This was proposed, among others, by such an eminent Catholic theologian as Melchior Cano, according to whom the partners' mutual consent to the marriage was the matter of the sacrament and the priest's blessing its form. Cano's book appeared in 1563, during the Council of Trent, and his view found many supporting theologians after the council and up to the 19th century.[5] While the sacrament was assigned to the power of the Church, the contract was to be an entirely non-religious matter, under the exclusive authority of the state. This doctrine was evolved completely only at the end of the 16th century, but its beginnings go far back. To the faithful at large such an idea might have seemed plausible because at that time the Church had not yet evolved an obligatory ecclesiastical marriage form. There existed a liturgical rite, but preceding this ceremony there was performed a juridical formality, often called betrothal, in front of or at the entrance of the Church (*in facie Ecclesiae*).

In this preliminary part the exchange of consent took place in the presence of authorized witnesses, who could be clergy, but very often were civil magistrates or notaries. Even when no liturgical blessing followed the exchange of consent, the pre-Tridentine Latin rite Church recognized the marriage as

---

tate to discard the opinion of Eugene IV, in the *Decree for the Armenians,* namely, that the entire, or at least the partial matter of the sacrament of orders consists in the transmission of the instruments, after he had with convincing evidence proved that the opinion was erroneous" (*Summa Theologiae Moralis,* pp. 28 and 729).

5. Schillebeeckx, *op. cit.,* pp. 372f.

valid if other requirements were observed. The faithful in general learned to see a marriage rite performed only in the presence of laymen as a marriage valid in the eyes of the Church and of God, and the subsequent liturgical rite as a legally inconsequential ceremony.

This apparent separation of marriage into two spheres, one —the legally important—belonging seemingly to the secular and another to the religious, was enhanced by the teaching of certain Reformers that the Church had nothing to do with marriage, except incidentally as an occasional delegate of the state.

The Council of Trent was convoked for the purpose of reforming the Church and for defining authoritatively the standpoint of the Church in opposition to Protestantism. We can therefore expect that the Council would counter the teaching of the Protestants in those aspects which Catholics regarded as erroneous, and would indicate, among other things, first: that marriage came under the exclusive authority of the Church and that the state possessed only the right to regulate the civil consequences of a marriage considered valid by the Church; and second: that only the Church possessed the right to determine the validity of marriage. This precluded also the possibility of divorce being allowed either by private authority or by grant of the secular power.

In interpreting the meaning of conciliar definitions, particularly those of Trent, it is necessary to know the teaching of those whose errors are rejected in the definition "Therefore, since it was the intention of the Fathers at Trent to refute the errors of the Protestants, and not the opinions which were freely discussed among Catholics, the canons will be naturally better understood if the errors of Luther and Calvin are diligently investigated." [6] We must also know what the Fathers wished to define, and what they intended to leave to free discussion. This will be known especially from the debates

6. A. Tanquerey, *Synopsis Theologiae Dogmaticae*, p. 649.

that preceded the definition and the acts of the council. And lastly, we must establish the meaning of the dogmatic terms at the time when the definition was adopted.

In order to separate marriage from civil interference, the council adopted an obligatory ecclesiastical marriage form, binding with the sanction of nullity wherever the decree *Tametsi* was promulgated.

On the question of divorce and remarriage, the following canon had been prepared and proposed to the Fathers of the Council:

Canon 6. If anyone shall say that marriage can be dissolved because of adultery of the other spouse, and that both spouses, or at least the innocent one who was not the cause of the adultery, are permitted to contract another marriage while the other spouse is alive; and that he who takes another, having dismissed the adulteress, or she who marries another, having dismissed the adulterer, does not commit adultery, let him be anathema.[7]

We are well informed of the respective debates which preceded the final promulgation of this canon, which later received the number seven.[8] It was a lengthy affair and only after protracted discussions was a formula found that satisfied, if not all, at least a majority of the Fathers. Had the Catholic doctrine on absolute indissolubility been really as established before Trent as so many Catholic theologians assert, this canon would have been formulated more readily.

Some bishops rejected the canon without reservations, because they saw in it a condemnation of the Fathers and

7. "Si quis dixerit, propter adulterium alterius coniugum posse matrimonium dissolvi, et utrique coniugum vel saltem innocenti, qui causam adulterio non dedit, licere, altero coniuge vivente, aliud matrimonium contrahere, neque moechari eum, qui dimissa adultera aliam duxerit, neque eam, quae dimisso adultero alii nupserit, anathema sit" (A. Massarello, *Acta Concilii Tridentini*, vol. II, p. 251).

8. For a description and bibliography, see the exhaustive but biased account and interpretation of A. Vacant ("Divorce," in *Dictionnaire*, vol. XII, cols. 498–505). See also G. H. Joyce, *Christian Marriage*, pp. 355ff.

especially of the Greek Church. They were headed by the Latin-rite Archbishop of the Greek Island of Crete, Pietro Laudi. Eighteen other bishops expressed the same opinion, but they would have accepted the canon if the anathema or condemnation of the Greek practice had been omitted. In other words, the character of a dogmatic decision would have been taken away from the canon. One of this group was the Archbishop of Rossano, Giovanni Battista Castagna, later Pope Urban VII (1590), who died only twelve days after his election. The Bishop of Segovia in Spain, Martin Perez de Ayala, criticized the proposed decree on the ground that one should not condemn the doctrine of several Fathers of the Church; and he suggested that instead it should be said that the Church did not err in teaching the indissolubility of the marriage. This was the formula which was ultimately adopted.

The Bishop of Modena, Egidio Foscarari, O.P., headed another group of bishops who proposed that the Council's anathema should be directed solely against those who deny the Church the right to prohibit remarriage in case of adultery. In other words, the dogmatic question would not be touched, but the discretionary power of the Church to forbid—and indirectly also to permit—total divorce would be affirmed. One can say, then, that the majority of the Fathers opposed the condemnation of the Greeks for one or the other reason.[9]

At this juncture the ambassadors of the Venetian Republic suggested that the language of the canon be changed to avoid offending the Greeks united with the Catholic Church in the domains of the Republic. The intervention was successful.[10] The Fathers accepted the idea originally proposed by the Bishop of Segovia, with one addition, that the teaching of the Church in this respect is "according to evangelical and apostolic doctrine." However, even in the new redaction the canon

9. A. Vacant, *art. cit.,* col. 499.

10. P. S. Pallavicino described the intervention of the Republic of Venice in the official history of the Council of Trent (*Istoria del Concilio di Trento,* vol. II), prepared at the order of Pope Alexander VII.

found a number of Fathers who rejected it up to the last voting, because they considered it not according to Sacred Scripture and the ancient Fathers of the Church, or they wished to see the condemnation of the Greek Church removed.

The final wording was adopted by majority vote in the fifth official session on this matter, the 24th public session of the Council, on November 11, 1563, with some two hundred Fathers participating:

Canon 7. If anyone shall say that the Church errs when she taught or teaches, in accordance with evangelical and apostolic doctrine, that the bond of marriage cannot be dissolved because of adultery of either spouse; and that neither of them, not even the innocent one who was not the cause of the adultery, can contract another marriage while the other spouse is living; and that he who has taken another after dismissing the adulteress; and she who has married another after dismissing the adulterer, commits adultery, let him be anathema." [11]

In his account of the manner in which the council arrived at the text of canon 7, Vacant also treats the question whether it is a disciplinary or a doctrinal canon. His conclusion is that it is a canon defining the absolute indissolubility of marriage as a doctrine of the Church. But he cannot pass over the fact that numerous Catholic theologians and canonists have disagreed during the first two centuries after Trent on this point. Perrone enumerates twenty-one of them,[12] but Vacant discards them with the remark that they were tainted with Gallicanism and Josephinism. The fact that these theologians promoted unorthodox ideas in other areas has no bearing, generally

---

11. Denzinger-Bannwart, *Enchiridion Symbolorum,* p. 977. Many will agree that this can be regarded as a typical intervention of divine Providence, guiding the Church towards the true doctrine: "Le S. Esprit n'aurait-il pas agi par les causes secondes (en l'occurence, l'intervention de Venise) pour protéger l'Eglise catholique d'un excès qui deviendrait une erreur et pour maintenir libre dans le catholicisme la place de la tradition orientale en la matière? En conscience, qui ne reconnaîtrait le droit de répondre négativement à pareille question?" (R. Clement, "Quelques questions à propos de la tradition orientale," p. 9).

12. *Op. cit.,* pp. 380ff.

speaking, in the province of marriage law. Their reasons for holding that canon 7 was not a doctrinal definition, was based on, among other things, the undeniable desire of the council to accommodate the Greeks, and to avoid condemning the ancient doctrine of celebrated Fathers of the Church.

The following possibility is here proposed, that the Council wished to define that the Church did not act wrongly and without justification in denying divorce. The decree was a vindication of the practice of the Church in denying divorce, and an affirmation that the Church possessed such power, which we refer to the power of the keys. Thereby the discipline of the Church became defined in respect to the past and the present. However, as in respect to all disciplinary laws, this did not exclude the possibility of a future change.[13]

Here the distinction should be introduced between intrinsic and extrinsic dissolubility. The Council can be presumed to have excluded and condemned, based upon the Gospel passages, intrinsic dissolubility, whether applied to a marriage by the contrahents themselves or by the secular power, even in the case of adultery. Yet, extrinsic dissolubility to be exercised by the Church as the sole authorized delegate of the legislator, that is, God, is thereby not excluded; it is simply not spoken of in canon 7.

It is also our opinion that the possibility ought to be considered that the Council simply was not successful in working out a clear and satisfactory definition. The discussions in the wake of the Second Vatican Council have familiarized us with the idea that even dogmatic definitions can be in need of correction as far as their linguistic form is concerned.[14] In

13. See R. Leys, "Is Teilhard Dangerous?", in *Theology Digest,* p. 39: "Later dogmatical formulations . . . are human words, the fruit of human reflection; and, though safeguarded from error by divine assistance, they are by no means to be considered inspired. So the dogmas are susceptible of a deepening of meaning or of an ever more precise formulation. To claim otherwise would be to render further theological reflection pointless."

14. ". . . if the influence of events or of the times has led to defi-

view of the disparate opinions, evidenced by the amount of work needed in the formulation of canon 7, it cannot be excluded *a priori* that the resulting compromise redaction is unsatisfactory, and that thereby an essential deficiency in the doctrinal definition suggests that one may regard canon 7 as a disciplinary decision.[15]

However, it has to be admitted that many Catholic theologians, perhaps most of them, accept canon 7 as a dogmatic definition that has terminated forever the question of a possible divorce of consummated sacramental marriages on account of adultery. We disagree with them for the following reasons:

(1) Teachers of dogmatic theology have admitted that the Council did not explicitly define the indissolubility of marriage. The direct object of the definition, according to their explanation, was the infallibility of the Church (*"Ecclesiam errare"*) and indissolubility is only the indirect object of canon 7. As a consequence, the indissolubility of marriage is not a dogmatic proposition *de fide,* but solely a proposition *fidei proxima.*[16] This was recognized even by such staunch defenders of the absolute indissolubility of marriage as F. Vogt, who only three decades ago lamented the "deficiency" of Trent: "From the standpoint of dogmatic theology, the keystone is still missing,

---

ciencies in conduct, in Church discipline, or even in the formulation of doctrine (which must be carefully distinguished from the deposit itself of faith), these should be appropriately rectified at the proper moment" (*Decree on Ecumenism*).

15. On the deficiencies in a non-dogmatic canonical decree of the Second Vatican Council, see V. J. Pospishil, *Orientalium Ecclesiarum: The Decree on the Eastern Catholic Churches of the Second Vatican Council.*

16. Perrone, *op. cit.,* pp. 407ff. F. Diekamp calls it a *sententia certa* (*Theologiae Dogmaticae Manuale,* vol. IV, p. 435). As a further corollary, he who denies that the indissolubility of marriage is a divinely revealed truth is not a heretic (see J. Pfab, *Aufhebung der ehelichen Lebensgemeinschaft nach göttlichem, kirchlichem und bürgerlichem Recht,* p. 63; Joyce, *op. cit.,* pp. 355ff.), although he may be sinning against obedience due to the Church, or even against the virtue of faith if the denial is advanced rashly, without sufficient evidence.

the crown for the entire edifice erected so far by her [the Church] for the realization of Christian marriage. This is especially true today regarding the doctrine of the absolute indissolubility of Christian marriage, which in virtue of the decision of Trent is not yet *de fide* but only in a *propositio fidei proxima,* in nothing else than a formal dogmatical declaration of the same." [17]

If one interprets the wording of canon 7 in a strict sense, it could be said that the Church did not define that she *cannot* dissolve marriage, but that, in refusing permission for divorce, and guided by the ideals set forth in the Gospels and the tradition of apostolic times, she has not erred in this matter. It can be inferred also that the Church could hypothetically err if she continues to deny divorce in spite of circumstances essentially different from those which existed when the previous norm was sanctioned.

(2) It can be admitted that the first redaction of canon 7, the original canon 6, would have terminated the discussion, and would have been a dogmatic decision forever excluding divorce on the ground of adultery. But this canon was not passed by the Council. Can it now be assumed that in spite of the change the Council still wished to say the same thing? Then what meaning and purpose would this change have had? [18] Can one believe that it involved solely a camouflage, whereby the same thing was said in another way, that deceptive circumlocution was employed? It seems more likely that the practice of the Greek Church had to be taken into consideration, and the dogmatic contents had to be changed accordingly. Neither can it be presumed that the Fathers were not aware of the doctrinal implication of the change. Since they intended to accommodate the Greeks because of their different practice,

17. *Das Ehegesetz Jesu,* p. 186. See also p. 51.
18. See Fahrner, *op. cit.,* p. 256: "If the Council Fathers had intended to define the principle of indissolubility itself as dogma, they would have kept the original wording of the canon."

namely, the concession of complete divorce, the definition of the Council could not have excluded the possibility of a hypothetical granting of divorce by the Catholic Church herself.

(3) At the same time, canon 5 was promulgated with this text:

Canon 5. If anyone shall say that the bond of matrimony can be dissolved for the cause of heresy, or of injury due to cohabitation, or of willful desertion, let him be anathema.[19]

Three reasons were expressly excluded as grounds for divorce: heresy, danger from cohabitation, as disease, infirmity, etc., and desertion. There is no mention of adultery, that ground which was most often advanced for divorce. This omission can hardly be explained as an oversight, for the Council wished to speak on that ground in a separate canon. The most obvious explanation for this omission is the persuasion of the Council that adultery could perhaps be a possible ground for total divorce. It is not implied that the Fathers were convinced that adultery permitted divorce, but solely that they were not sure one could apodictically exclude it.

(4) One can accept the explanation that the infallibility of the Church in the matter of divorce had been defined, but with this qualification: that the Church has not erred in denying the possibility of divorce as it was demanded by those against whom the Council had been convoked, and within the limits dictated by these needs. Protestant teaching relegated marriage and the right of granting divorce to the state. This was at that time the only teaching concerning divorce, and in order to oppose this specific teaching canon 7 was passed by the Council. In other words, the Council did not define that the Church could not grant divorce. At that time nobody had advanced this thought in the Western Church with any per-

19. "Si quis dixerit propter haeresim aut molestam cohabitationem aut affectatam absentiam a coniuge dissolvi posse matrimonii vinculum, anathema sit" (Denzinger, 975).

71

sistence, and there was no reason why the Council should take cognizance of such a possibility.

Since there was no provocation to deny this power to the Church, no dogmatic definition was necessary. There was simply no reason whatever why the Church should define her alleged inability, limit her own authority. The attention of the Council Fathers was directed towards the claims of the secular power. Nobody had actually at that time demanded from the Church the right to grant divorces. There was thus no cause for defining something which had not been challenged.

The often passionate language used in ecclesiastical pronouncements since Trent against the doctrine of divorce becomes plausible only if we know that the Church directed it against the claims of the secular power, which were supported by Protestant teaching, to grant divorce decrees. This kind of language would be unnecessary and unnatural if it were directed against the doctrine which denied such authority to the state but assigned it to the Catholic Church.

When the Council therefore emphasized that the Church did not err in forbidding any dissolution of a consummated Christain marriage, it was motivated mainly by the need to exclude the secular power from the marriage law. This the Council did first by establishing an ecclesiastical form for the marriage contract, obligatory under pain of nullity (*Tametsi*), and then by taking away from the state the right of dissolving such a contract, by affirming that the Church had not erred in refusing divorce. If the Church did not grant true divorces, then much less could the state.

(5) Why should the Church condemn a teaching when those who advance it would subject its exercise entirely to the authority of the Church? This teaching which is here proposed was then not yet existing. Those Western theologians or canonists of the times who did not reject divorce assigned the right of administering this authority either to the state alone, as the Protestants did, or to the Church and state on

72

equal terms, as some Catholics did who distinguished in marriage the contract from the sacrament. Cajetan and Catharinus saw a possibility of divorce in the New Testament, but they said nothing concerning who would have jurisdiction over it. No doctrinal decision, coming from a council or a pope, infallible or otherwise, can refer to a possible future, not yet existing, teaching.

6. PENITENTIALS AND FORMULARIES

An important source for the study of the marriage law of the Church during the centuries of the invasion of the barbaric Germanic tribes in Western Europe are the penitential books. The first centuries of Christianity did not yet know the practice of frequent confession. Baptism was often delayed to an advanced age, sometimes to the hour of death, in order to receive the benefit of a total remission of sins and punishment. Public confession and concomitant penance were prescribed for the three capital sins: apostasy, murder, and adultery.

The change of ecclesiastical discipline after the Church had achieved freedom and then a privileged status in the Roman Empire led slowly to specific confession of all sins and to private confession even of secret transgressions. Since the idea continued that the kind and amount of penance ought specifically be adapted to each sin, the task of the priest increased in complexity and difficulty. It therefore became necessary for him in the administration of the sacrament of penance to have some guidelines for his decision as to what kind and what degree of severity of punishment should be imposed. The aim was to come to a clear notion of the various sins and their species, of their relative grievousness and importance, and of the appropriate expiatory punishment for each. In order to ensure uniform procedure, it was necessary for the Church authorities to lay down more detailed directions. This was done especially in the form of replies to specific inquiries

73

addressed to men renowned for their learning, first a number of Fathers, as Cyprian of Carthage, Basil of Cappadocia, Gregory of Nyssa, Peter of Alexandria, and others, followed by decrees of popes, often in the form of letters, and finally of canons of synods.

While it was easy to manage the spiritual affairs of the new believers in the time of persecution, who had entered the Church out of the loftiest motives, it became a more difficult task when it became advantageous or even necessary to be a member of the Church. This transformation of the quality of members was even more pronounced with the conversion of the barbarians in Western Europe.

It was now necessary to include in the catalogue of sins many new kind of crimes, which often mirrored the different moral and legal concepts of these nations, and to devise corresponding penances for each of them. To make application of all the penitential norms possible, the various dicta of Fathers, the decisions of popes and patriarchs, as well as the canons of various synods, were since the sixth century collected into penitential books.[1] They were first begun to be used in the Irish-Scottish Church and were then by their missionary and nomadic bishops transplanted over all of Western Europe. Their greatest development fell between 650 and 800. The Carolingian reform synods (Tours, Chalons, 813; Paris, 829; Mainz, 847; etc.) opposed, banned, and burned them, because too much arbitrariness had crept into the penitentials of that epoch. However, new collections of penitentials continued to come out and to be used. Bishops of the ninth and tenth centuries often demanded that pastors prove the possession of a penitential to the archdeacon at the time of the canonical visitation of the parish, and confessors were required to hear the confession of the faithful with a penitential in their hands.

These penitential books were an intentional adaptation to

---

1. G. Le Bras, "Penitentiels," in *Dictionnaire*, vol. XII, cols. 1158-1579. See also H. J. Schmitz, *Die Bussbücher und die Bussdisziplin der Kirche*.

the exigencies of the new situation in which the Church found itself. While it was impossible, for example, in the orderly provinces of the old Roman Empire of the third and fourth centuries to conceive that large numbers of citizens would be abducted by marauders, this became a normal occurrence in the Gaul of the seventh or eight centuries. It became thereby imperative for the Church to take cognizance of such problems as whether a husband whose wife had been carried off could marry another woman, and what should be done if the first wife returned, and so forth.

This adaptation to the realities of life can be viewed as a relaxation of Church discipline, or even laxism, only if we start with the assumption that it was the decree of the Founder of the Church that there cannot be any divorce and remarriage. This assumption is made by many Catholic students of Church history. However, if we stand upon the tradition of all the Eastern Churches, then the development of Church discipline in respect to marriage, as evidenced in the penitential books, will appear as a normal historical development, as a harmonious and parallel evolution of principles always present in the Church.

The penitentials reached also the Eastern Church, especially the Slavic Orthodox Churches in Ukraine-Russia. It is not sure whether they were brought there in the ninth century by SS. Cyril and Methodius or at a later date.[2] But because of the substantial identity of the discipline of the Western and Eastern Churches at that time, especially in the question of divorce, acceptance of the penitentials in the East should have been easy.

The various passages from penitentials have been discussed in this book under the names of the respective author, as, for example, those ascribed to a number of synods held in Gaul, such as Arles, Compiegne, etc., or St. Theodore of Canterbury, and others. They permit remarriage for various reasons. It is

2. Noonan, *Contraception,* p. 167, n. 23.

not our contention that the penitentials simply teach the possibility of divorce and remarriage; for while it was often permitted, a clear doctrine on the dissolubility of marriage is not defined. For our purpose, to show that this problem was not resolved, and the discussion considered definitely closed, it is sufficient to offer proof that these documents actually in various instances expressly permitted divorce and remarriage. This is adequate evidence that men, dedicated to God and the Church, did not consider the question adjudicated or divorce against the salvific plan of Christ.

The gradual disappearance of public penance, and the reform movement beginning in the tenth century, made the penitential books obsolete and they vanished. It was also the time when the universities were founded in Western Europe, and provided the Church with systematic textbooks on moral theology.

To the same category as the penitentials belong the so-called formularies, collections of public and private documents for the use of notaries and other legal administrators. In the matter of divorce grounds they are the most liberal witnesses of all times, permitting consensual divorce without any limitation, as can be seen in the *Formularies of Angers* (sixth century) and the *Formularies of Marculf* (seventh century).

7. CONCLUSION:
THE CASE OF USURY—INTEREST

In concluding this survey it is necessary to point briefly to one of the strongest historical parallels of the clarification of religious doctrine: the case of usury.

Here is a precedent which in every instance is almost identical with our own problem: strong belief in a scriptural foundation, persuasion that the expressions of the Fathers supported it, decrees of synods and popes excluding it absolutely and forever, solid reasons advanced by theologians, and so forth.

Ancient philosophers such as Plato, Aristotle, Seneca, and Plutarch, disapproved of interest, and considered it opposed to the nature of things.

The Old Testament, mirroring the circumstances of an agrarian society, permitted interest for loans only to non-Israelites: "You shall not lend upon interest to your brother, interest on money, interest on victuals, interest on anything that is lent for interest. To a foreigner you may lend upon interest, but to your brother you shall not lend upon interest; . . ." (Deut. 23, 19–20).

The New Testament mentions the practice of the time of Jesus of lending money to bankers at interest (Mt. 25, 27; Lk. 19, 23) with no disapproval, although it is clear that the bankers could pay the interest only if they had loaned the same money to others at a higher rate of interest. The passage of Luke (6, 34), "And if you lend to those from whom you hope to receive, what credit is that to you? Even sinners lend to sinners, to receive as much again," was by some interpreted as condemnation of interest; although it is only an exhortation to benevolence, an ideal to be voluntarily followed rather than a legal norm to be observed under sanction.

It was generally believed, even by such a renowned canonist as Pope Benedict XIV (Prosper Lambertini),[1] that the testimony of the Fathers supported the absolute prohibition. However, in studying the relevant passages one comes to the conclusion, identical to that which was made in reference to the prohibition of divorce, that the Christian writers of the first centuries merely inveighed against avarice and usury and exploitation of misfortune, and that they supported their teaching with references to passages of Scripture. As with divorce, the Fathers were more concerned with elevating the aspirations of Christians than with defining obligatory legal or moral rules.

Similarly, the condemnation of interest by various synods

1. *De synodo dioecesana,* X, IV, n. 6.

has to be examined closely. Most of them denounced the acceptance of interest by members of the clergy.[2] Only I Carthage (345) and Aix (789) seems to have forbidden the taking of interest by laymen as well. Leo I declared in his letter *Nec hoc quoque* that clerics were absolutely forbidden to take interest, while laymen who took it were said to be guilty of seeking shameful gain.[3]

However, again in remarkable parallelism with the problem of divorce, from the eleventh century on the canon law of the Western Church absolutely forbade interest on loans, as is evidenced in several places in Gratian's Decree and in the Decretals. Pope Alexander III (1159–1181), who as Rolando Baldinelli was one of the great canonists of his time, declared in a decree [4] that he as pope had no power to dispense from this prohibition. The Ecumenical Council of Vienne in France (1311) declared that if anyone should obstinately maintain that there was no sin in the practice of demanding interest, he should be punished as heretic.[5] Any interest, moderate or excessive, was branded as usury; even credit sales at a price higher than the cash price were considered usurious, and the Church could not relax the prohibition even to raise money for such a worthy cause as is the ransoming of Christian captives from the Saracens.[6]

Urban III (1185–1187) cited in his letter *Consuluit* [7] the words of Jesus, "lend, expecting nothing in return" (Lk. 6, 35), as a specific command of Christ that was authoritatively interpretated by the pope as forbidding usury and the taking of any interest as an absolute divine prohibition.

2. J. S. Pitra, *Iuris ecclesiastici Graecorum historia et monumenta*, vol. I, p. 24.

3. Noonan, *The Scholastic Analysis of Usury*, p. 15

4. *Decretales*, 1, V, tit. XIX, col. 4; Noonan, *Usury*, p. 19.

5. "Si quis in illum errorem inciderit ut pertinaciter affirmare praesumpserit exercere usuras non esse peccatum, decernimus eum velut haereticum puniendum" (Denzinger, 479).

6. Noonan, *Usury*, p. 19.

7. *Decretales*, V, 19, 10.

Theologians of succeeding centuries were also in general accord that every advantage accruing to the lender, either in money, that is, interest proper, or in services rendered by the borrower, above the sum originally loaned, was usury. Thus usury was condemned by holy Scripture, moral theology, and natural, civil, and ecclesiastical law.

However, again with amazing analogy to the absolute condemnation of divorce, a lack of congruence was permitted to exist, in that the Jews were exempt from this prohibition—although some synods and popes extended the prohibition to them also. But the economic needs of society could not be overlooked. As with divorce, it was still difficult—and is to the present day—to determine the boundary between usury and just interest, precisely as it seems now to be impossible to establish the exact limits between equitable and unjustified grounds for divorce.

The great scholastics evolved several distinctions between various kinds of loans, and these were further refined by succeeding generations of theologians, so that today it is permitted to loan money for interest on account of several external titles: loss of earning in another possible undertaking (*lucrum cessans*); pecuniary loss because of impossibility to make use of one's money in an emergency (*damnum emergens*); danger of losing the money loaned (*periculum sortis*); moratory payment in case the loan is not repaid on time (*poena conventionalis*).

New ideas, formulated in the wake of Renaissance, and circulated by a few legal thinkers, were gathered into a new theory by Calvin, who denied that money was in itself sterile and unproductive. In his commentary on Ezekiel and in his letter to Oecolampadius, Calvin proposed that interest is permissible if it is not excessive and if it is not demanded from the poor. This new teaching was not, however, taken up immediately either by Catholic or Lutheran theologians.

The European economy continued its phenomenal development during the following centuries while completely ignoring

Catholic teaching, which seemed to have no connection with reality. Scipio Maffei (1675–1755), a banker and businessman of Verona and a personal friend of Benedict XIV, stepped into the controversy which had developed over the question whether a 4 per cent interest on a Veronese bond issue was morally permissible. Maffei's book in defense of taking interest provoked the Roman Curia to prevail upon the Pope to issue the encyclical letter *Vix Pervenit* (1745).[8] It did not contain any appeal to papal infallibility, but it was considered to be a dogmatic judgment, and had the appearance of being a definitive doctrinal decision. The Pope declared it to be sinful to reclaim anything above the sum advanced for the loan itself (*ex ipso mutuo . . . ipsius ratione mutui*). He added that it was immaterial whether the surcharge above the original loan were moderate or large, or whether the borrower were rich or poor, or whether he would make use of the loan for some lucrative business transaction or leave it unused. But not even Roman circles were sure and unanimous in what actually had been condemned in the encyclical, and the confusion was compounded when Maffei republished his book with the imprimatur of the Master of the Sacred Palace, the highest authority for censorship in Rome.

As was forseeable, this decision did not resolve the problem, and economic theory and practice, in Catholic and non-Catholic nations alike, ignored it. In 1830, the Holy Office and the Sacred Penitentiary replied to inquiries that Catholic penitents who accept moderate interest and are ready to abide by a final decision of the Church need not be disturbed in their conscience. The Sacred Penitentiary proposed in 1889 as guideline for Catholics to follow the usage accepted among honest men.[9]

Thus, after an impassioned discussion of more than one thousand years it became clear that "taking of interest" and

8. Denzinger, 1475-1978.
9. A. Bernard, G. Le Bras, H. Du Passage, "Usure," in *Dictionnaire*, vol. XV, part 2, cols. 2316-2390.

"usury" are not the same; while the latter remained forbidden, the former was allowed. As to the boundaries between them, the example of conscientious men was to be decisive.

The same is here proposed in respect to the question of permissibility of total divorce: let the teaching of the past be examined, and when it is recognized that there is no irreversible decision of the Church involved, let the problem be submitted to an earnest review. In case it appears impossible to draw the line between what can be permitted in respect to divorce and remarriage, and what is to be refused, let the conscience of dedicated members of the Church be decisive.

III.

DIVORCE AND
CONTEMPORARY LIFE

1. THE DEMANDS OF THE PRESENT

OF special concern to the Church today are the many Catholics who have separated from their marriage partners, have obtained a civil divorce, and have remarried, either before a non-Catholic minister of religion or before a civil magistrate.

These members of the Church incur the following penalties and disabilities, which we shall list serially in order that their severity can be fully appreciated.

Up to the recent decree of Pope Paul VI, such Catholics were automatically excommunicated if they contracted a new marriage before a non-Catholic minister (canon 2319, #1, n. 1). In some dioceses also a marriage before a civil magistrate was punished by excommunication.

They could be suspect of heresy (canon 2319, # 2; 2316).

Because of their living together with a new marriage partner without the approval of the Church, they are public sinners.

The civil marriage contracted by them is in Church law not even considered an invalid marriage, but no marriage at all, since it lacks the legal appearance (*species et forma*) of a marriage.

They are not to be admitted as sponsors (godparents) at a baptism or confirmation (canon 766, n. 2).

They cannot receive a Christian burial in a Catholic cemetery, and cannot be buried by the Church, and no memorial service can be publicly celebrated for them (canon 1240, # 1, n. 6; 1241).

They cannot receive sacraments, that is, especially cannot

be absolved in confession except if they promise either to separate from each other, or to live as brother and sister, provided the circumstances are such that no scandal is given to other members of the Church—that is, it must be virtually unknown—and that there is a likelihood that the promise will be kept, which in effect means that the individuals are quite elderly.

They, as bigamists, incur the penalty of legal infamy (can. 2356).

They are to be deprived of certain sacramentals (blessings), as that given to a mother after the birth and baptism of a child (canon 2291, n. 6).

They are forbidden to exercise so-called legitimate acts (canon 2375), such as being members of church management boards, acting as attorney in ecclesiastical courts, and so forth.

In spite of the fact that they incur all these punishments, they do not cease to be members of the Church and are obliged to fulfill all their duties towards the Church (canon 87), such as that of financial support.

The Church is the organization placed by God in charge of securing the salvation of her members here on earth. It is theoretically immaterial whether a certain measure of ecclesiastical administration affects the good of one soul only or of millions: the Church is concernd with each single individual. However, in the pressure of daily business it is understandable that the leaders of the Church must decide which problems are more important, and therefore require immediate attention, and how many individual members will be affected by the judgments of authority.

It will be therefore of some importance to know how great is the number of Catholics who are directly involved in the issue of divorce. While all alert Catholics, especially the clergy, are aware that the problem of Catholics living in invalid marriages is numerically significant, nobody can cite any dependable statistics. It should not be too difficult to gather such statistics in nations where the great majority of the population are Catholics, and where civil divorce can be obtained by every citizen without special difficulty; in such cases, the number of marriages or divorces, as reported by the state authorities, needs little correction to apply to all Catholics. In other nations, religious aspects of statistical occurrences are intentionally ignored, either because of the disinterestedness or animosity of the state towards the Church, or in order not to infringe upon the principle of separation of state and Church; this latter is the situation in the United States and Great Britain.

Despite these difficulties, we shall attempt to compute in a loose fashion the roughly approximate number of Catholics affected by invalid unions in the United States as well as in some other countries.

The number of divorces reported annually in the United States in recent years has passed 400,000, and in 1965 had reached 430,000.[1] The Catholic population of the U. S. amounts now to 46 million in a total of 190 million, or close to 25 per cent. Divorces among Catholics will be somewhat fewer partly on account of the negative attitude of the Church towards divorce and partly because of the relatively uniform social mores of American Catholics, most of whom belong to the so-called lower middle class.[2] However, a circumstance favoring

1. The U.S. Public Health Service published figures on the divorce rate showing a constant increment, from 368,000 in 1959 to 413,000 in 1962. The number of divorces per 1,000 population remained approximately the same: 2.2 in 1962. According to this ratio we may deduce, without any adjustment of figures, that there were, in 1964, 101,200 divorces in a Catholic population of 46 million.

2. Catholics in Philadelphia, Pa., had in the 1950's only one-half to two-thirds of the divorce rate which might have been expected from their proportion in the population (W. M. Kephart, *The Family, Society and the Individual,* p. 608). However, the equalization of the U.S. population and the increasing elimination of religious influence in public life will narrow down the difference in divorce rate between Catholics and non-Catholics.

P. H. and P. F. Jacobson have come to the same conclusion: "There are indications that the recorded rate for legal dissolutions is lower among Catholics than among the population as a whole. However, it is

divorce among Catholics is that most of them live in the large cities of the nation, where divorces occur more often than in rural communities. In 1956, 19.4 per cent of Catholics were classified as rural (farm and non-farm), while in the entire U. S. population the proportion was 43 per cent rural—and of that figure, only 8 per cent were Catholic. With continued urbanization and flight from the farm, this proportion has since diminished.[3]

It may reasonably be assumed, therefore, that the number of Catholic couples who terminate their marriage by divorce every year is around 70,000. If we say, then, that they have thirty years of married life still before them,[4] we could say also that there are approximately 2,100,000 Catholic couples or 4,200,000 individual Catholics living either in invalid marriages or in obligatory isolation. Of course, nobody has ever had the experience that 10 per cent of the congregation or parish to which he belongs in a Catholic town or city are divorced. However, let us not forget that most of the Catholics living in marital unions considered invalid by the Church have left the Catholic community, either to join non-Catholic religious denominations, or to live without any religious practice.

John L. Thomas, S. J.,[5] offers similar data on the basis of a study involving 24,338 Catholic families in 18 suburban parishes. Of these, 5678 were invalid marriages; or in other words,

---

possible that religious differences have been decreasing" (*American Marriage and Divorce*, p. 101).

3. J. L. Thomas, *The American Catholic Family*, p. 284.

4. The median age for U.S. couples, including here divorced and widowed persons: if both spouses have been married previously, 42 years for men, 37 for women; if the husband is marrying for the first time while the wife is remarrying, 29; if husband is remarrying while it is the first marriage for her, 33. If these statistics would exclude remarriage of widowed persons, who are on the average older, the median age for these three categories (both remarrying, man remarrying, and woman remarrying) would be correspondingly lower (see P. C. Glick, *American Families. A Volume in the Census Monograph Series*, p. 114).

5. *Op. cit.*, p. 166.

23.5 per cent. However, we can apply certain corrections, as the presumption that some of these invalid marriages could have been convalidated, and therefore do not belong in our category, and that the proportion of invalid marriages in a suburban population, on account of the greater incidence of mixed marriages, can be expected to be greater than in city parishes. The same author reports that the Bishops' Committee estimated that each year "between 15 and 25 per cent of all marriages involving Catholics are invalid." [6] This situation has certainly not abated, but rather is on the increase.

William J. Goode estimated that 17 to 20 per cent of all men and women in the United States will experience divorce in their lifespan.[7] In a population of two hundred million, this would amount to at least 11 to 13 million marriages.[8]

6. *Ibid.*
7. *After Divorce*, p. 11.
8. Glick (*op. cit.*) makes use of the data furnished by the 1950 U.S. census, and comes to various interesting conclusions: Two-thirds of the women and three-thirds of the men who obtain a divorce will eventually remarry (p. 139). Divorces were most likely to occur during the second or third year of marriage (p. 140). One-half of those obtaining a divorce or an annulment did so during the first six years of marriage (p. 140). Fifty per cent of couples obtaining a divorce (in 22 states) had no children (p. 140). There were more marriages in 1953 between a single person and a divorced person than marriages of two divorced persons, and more marriages of a divorced person and a widowed person than marriages of two divorced persons (p. 199). Second marriages are quite stable: about seven out of every eight who remarry are entering their second marriage, and only two or three per cent of all marriages are contracted by persons entering their third or a subsequent marriage. This includes also the marriages of widowed persons (p. 199). For divorced persons who remarried during the early 1950's the median time elapsing between the dissolution of the previous marriage and remarriage was about two and a half years (p. 198). Glick also concludes that the high remarriage rate of many decades "in itself does not mean our society is unstable. Perhaps divorce is generally less a repudiation of marriage than an expression of dissatisfaction with a particular marriage partner" (p. 135).

Thomas (*op. cit.*) also makes several interesting statements relevant to our topic: In general, the first five years of marriage eliminated most of the initially unstable unions (p. 264). Between 1940 and 1950, valid mixed marriages constituted 25 to 30 per cent of all Catholic

Some might object that these enormous numbers go far beyond what they ever imagined. Even if one would apply such a "correction" as to halve the above figure of divorced Catholics, because Catholics are regarded—mistakenly, though —more immune against divorce and remarriage temptations than other Americans, the number is appalling and the problem appears in all its overwhelming magnitude.

To this huge number there have to be added the ten thousands of Catholics who marry non-Catholics, themselves divorced. These marriages also cannot be celebrated in Church if the non-Catholic and his or her first spouse were baptized.

The number of Catholics contracting marital unions in the United States which are not recognized as marriages by the Church can be established with considerable accuracy from another source, namely, the *Statistical Abstracts of the United States for 1965,* published by the U. S. Department of Commerce. The marriage rate of the U. S. in 1965 per 1,000 population was 9.0, and the actual number of all marriages was projected as 1,720,000. For the same year the *Official Catholic Directory for the United States* reports 342,458 marriages witnessed by Catholic priests. There is no reason to believe that the Catholic population of 45,640,000 differs in the frequency of marriages from the rest of the U. S. Had all

---

marriages (p. 154). There is good reason to believe that this rate will gradually increase (p. 169). In the whole of the United States, two-thirds of all divorces took place within the first ten years of marriage, and 80 per cent within the first fifteen years (p. 207).

In his study on divorce, Goode (*op. cit.*) comes to various conclusions which bear on our problem. With reference to a statistical study on divorce in Detroit in 1952, he says of Catholics: "As can be seen, however, the contribution to the total divorced population is not much less than their proportion of the total population" (p. 36). Even if it is true that Catholics ultimately remarry in as high a proportion as Protestants, perhaps they take longer to get married (p. 277). About 94 per cent of all women divorced at age 30 will remarry (p. 277). As to happiness found in remarriage, a study showed that there are no real differences by religion, although Catholics seem very slightly more inclined (92 vs. 84 per cent) to say that second marriages are much better (p. 335).

Catholics contracted Catholic marriages, the number should have been 410,760. In other words: some 68,000 Catholics married outside the Church.

Whatever criticism anybody would want to apply to this manner of conjecturing statistics, the point remains that there can be no doubt that in a nation such as the United States, the number of Catholics living in marriages which the Church condemns as invalid is going into the millions.

Moreover, even this number does not include all unsuccessful marriages, for there must also be taken into consideration the number of informal separations, usually statistically gathered under the heading of "deserted spouses." According to the Catholic sociologist Joseph T. Alves, the proportion of divorces to desertions among U. S. Catholics is 40 per cent to 60 per cent.[9] W. M. Kephart reports the same statistics for Philadelphia in 1955, namely, a proportion of two to three, or of broken marriages 40 per cent had ended in divorce and 60 per cent were in desertion.[10] While this seems to lower the number of divorces for Catholics in comparison with the higher percentage among non-Catholics, Catholics have a higher rate of desertion, as Kephart discovered in Philadelphia.[11]

9. "It is now estimated that more than 40 per cent of all marital dissolutions result from divorce. If one adds to the number of divorces annually the number of desertions, a growing phenomenon in American society about which little has been writen or said, the rate of which some authorities believe to be at least half as high as the divorce rate, and includes as well the number of annulments, one is brought to face with the alarming fact that America has now the unenviable record of having approximately one-third of its marriages end in failure . . ." ("Consequences of Marriage Breakdown," p. 203).

10. Op. cit., p. 548.

11. "The most extensive data concerning the religious factor in desertion is to be found in the annual reports of the Philadelphia Municipal Court. For some forty years the religious affiliation of both husband and wife has been recorded as an official part of the desertion-record form. The general picture is similar to that reported above. Court records indicate that, from 1915 down to the present, Catholics are over-represented and Jews and Protestants under-represented in white desertion cases. . . . Catholics, estimated at about 40 per cent

It is not surprising, then, that Thomas P. Monahan noted in 1955: "The combined figure of all existing families which are socially in conflict or disrupted is probably around 10 per cent . . . Their number is much greater than is generally realized by the community or by professional persons." [12] One could concede that this 10 per cent might be a little lower for Catholic families, but on the other hand it does not include families of those Catholics who have remarried. They do not figure in Monahan's statistics as disrupted, but for our purpose they are still spiritually divided and in religious conflict.

The problem of unstable marriages of teenagers is also increasing every day. Of the 430,000 annual divorces in 1965 in the U. S., 45 per cent were of marriages originally entered into by girls still in their teen years. In summary, no matter what statistics are used, the problem of Catholics living in invalid marriages is constantly increasing in a greater percentage than the Catholic population as such.

Similar statements could be made for every nation, especially for such "Catholic" countries as France, and in particular all the South American nations.[13] The complete breakdown of stable family life in the Latin American countries has been the object of study by anthropologists for some decades. It is not intended to treat this problem here, but if there is any solution to it in these nominally Catholic countries, one aspect

---

of the white population, were involved in some 60 per cent of the white desertion cases" (*ibid.*, p. 555).

12. Quoted *ibid.*, p. 543.

13. Landy has made a study of some villages in Puerto Rico with these results: Although nearly the entire population professes the Catholic faith, only 22 per cent of the marriages were blessed in church, 45 per cent were contracted before a civil magistrate, 27 per cent were consensual or common law marriages, and six per cent were contracted in a Protestant ceremony (*Tropical Childhood. Cultural Transmission and Learning in a Rural Puerto Rican Village*, p. 70).

The American anthropologist Oscar Lewis is renowned for his study of the Mexican family in which the instability of the marital union is the most remarkable feature (see for example his *Anthropology of Poverty: Five Families, La Vida,* and *Life in a Mexican Village*).

of it would certainly be a doctrinal change of the attitude of the Church towards divorce.

The number of divorces in 1962 in the Federal Republic of Germany (West Germany) was 49,521.[14] Catholics are now approximately one half of the population. Taking into account that the divorces among Protestants might be higher, it shall be assumed the number of Catholic divorces is around 20,000; and employing the same criteria as for the U. S., we arrive at 600,000 couples or 1,200,000 individual divorced Catholics.

How little help the Church has to offer today to these lost sheep is apparent when one reads the views of a recognized expert on the problem. Bernard Häring, in *Marriage in the Modern World,* has a special chapter titled "Pastoral Care for Remarried Divorced Persons," [15] and to couples in this situation he can offer only such inadequate comforts as: their union ought not be called concubinage; one cannot demand in every case of an invalid marriage and in all circumstances that the couple must separate; that they not be disturbed if they are sincerely convinced that a former marriage was invalid and therefore believe that their present one is valid; brother-sister arrangements can be permitted even if the couple has not entirely succeeded in living together without having sexual intercourse.

It would seem that the only practical remedy for this catastrophe is the acceptance of divorce by the Church. However, until the theoretical reflections have been worked out by the theologians which will permit the Church to effect such a doctrinal change, it will be necessary to impress the authorities of the Church with the magnitude of the problem. Catholics living in such invalid unions will have to come forward and express themselves before the hierarchy and clergy. It could even be proposed that these Catholics should organize themselves in each diocese in order to make the Church aware of their plight. They should not agitate as militant pressure

14. H. Flatten, *Das Aergernis der kirchlichen Eheprozesse,* p. 15.
15. Pp. 301-304.

90

groups, because they ought to know that the Church, composed of human beings, needs time to change, and that without a preceding doctrinal clarification and adjustment no legal modification can be expected. It will require time before Catholic theologians recognize that they have ignored the fundamental distinction between intrinsic and extrinsic dissolubility in respect to marriage, and that they have assigned to the Church far too little power. What all Catholics, also those living in good, stable Catholic marriages, ought to support is a demand submitted to the Church that the question be earnestly studied, without the usual bias by the traditionalists in authority.[16] The final and decisive say will, of course, be reserved to the magisterium of the Church.

2. THE RELEVANCE OF SOCIOLOGY AND PSYCHOLOGY

In its treatment of the individual and of the individuality of each human personality, the marriage law of the Catholic Church, so we have seen, appears to be too rigid. This law presumes that there is a human nature which remains uninfluenced and unshaped by the forces of environment, and that therefore the same rules that might have been justified in some specific circumstances of the Middle Ages apply equally to the complex human situation of twentieth-century urban life.

Yet the moral theology of the Catholic Church, which has been characterized as inflexible in the application of its norms, has a built-in principle of development. It is true that principles of moral theology, when they define what will be sinful and what meritorious in the conduct of men, have as subject an imaginary man, actually a phantom composed solely of in-

16. ". . . there is always a strong tendency to narrow down far too closely the range of what parts of the Faith can legitimately be discussed. Any such narrowing-down does not in fact help to keep the Faith strong and secure" (K. Rahner, *Free Speech in the Church*, p. 27).

tellect and will and untouched by environmental forces originating in his body or impinging from the surrounding milieu; however, moral theology adds at once that all the personal peculiarities of a human subject of the law must be taken into consideration when the imputability of an act is to be established. For example, a person whose body has a physiological predeterminant to alcoholism whether hereditary or acquired will incur a lesser guilt or imputability if he sins by excessive drinking than one who is free of such a restriction. Moral theology, in other words, seeks to assure each man of a just treatment, exactly measured to his unique, individual nature and constitution.

Canon law, on the contrary, ignores individual differences. It pays attention to certain external facts, as that the marriage contract was entered into in the presence of a representative of the Church and witnesses, or that the contract does not bind someone subject to certain kinds of fear; but beyond such macroscopic limitations little attention is given to individual inequalities.

Yet obviously such inequalities do exist. We are, for example, now living in the era of mass media. A child born today in an American, Canadian, British, or German home will be exposed to the influences of the mores concerning marriage of his society from the very dawn of his intellectual life. The media, particularly television, will bring it into every home every day of the year. The media may not propagate divorce directly, but only show it as appropriate and normal in various marital situations. Such a conditioning will then be intensified by other influences, as when the individual is made aware of the frequency of divorce and remarriage among the prominent people of his country, people who in other respects call forth his admiration.

Naturally, he is also exposed to the indoctrination of the Church and is made aware of the sinfulness, not so much of divorce, as of remarriage. And when he finally himself contracts a marriage, he wishes it to last until the end of his life and that it be a Catholic, indissoluble marriage. However, when serious and overwhelming trials disturb his plans for the future, he will face temptations which men born in another age never even dreamt of. But the law of the Church will not take heed of his plea that he is different in the make-up of his personality from a Catholic raised in another environment.

A sensible understanding of the nature of salvation history would suggest that the Church, in the name of the Creator of human nature, should regard it as her sacred trust to regulate the inflexibility of the law in such a way as to accommodate it to the exigencies of times and persons. This might mean today a mitigation; but, hypothetically speaking, it does not exclude also the possibility that the Church could also make more rigorous the rules of law in the future.

The ease with which marriages are entered into today by teenagers, to take one example to which we adverted above, ought to be reflected in the laws of the Church. She is called by her Founder to extend her help to those who are in distress even when they are themselves the indirect causes of their predicament. However, it can be questioned how much blame is to be put on young people for immature marriages and divorces particularly if they have been unprotected against the kind of upbringing previously described. It is not the task of the Church to rebuke these young people, but to offer them her assistance.

Whether a couple will be able to overcome their disruptive tendencies will depend, therefore, on the amount of social pressure felt by them to conform to the mores of the community. If separation, divorce, and remarriage are frowned upon, perhaps to the extent that it is regarded as utterly abominable, then it will be, psychologically speaking, easier for them to adjust. Should, however, the attitude of the social environment be one of tolerance towards those who resort to divorce and remarriage, the temptation to follow their example will be much stronger. Bernard Häring has expressed this weakening of the protective social forces in this way: "The fact that in earlier times the possibility of divorce did not loom on the horizon, neither at the time of marriage nor later when difficulties and crises arose, not only was a buttress for marriage outwardly as a matter of fate or force, but also helped the individual to an easier understanding of its essence and meaning. The natural tensions were dealt with in an entirely different way from the start." [1]

There can be no doubt that even in countries which are considered truly Catholic, divorce and remarriage of Catholics are not condemned with the same severity as in previous times. The social isolation of Catholics has mostly broken down, not the least because of the increasing number of mixed marriages. More and more Catholics resolve their marital difficulties by imitating the secularized majority of non-Catholics, agnostics, or disbelievers, and thereby they change the sociopsychological environment of every other Catholic by proffering their own example of remarriage. Catholics have also become aware that their Church does not abhor divorce, because they have with increasing frequency heard that the Roman Pontiff grants dispensative dissolutions to natural marriages, even to those which were entered in the Catholic Church (Fresno Cases). Nor can one discount all the rumors most Catholics have heard of annulments of marriages of heads of states and their relatives.

In spite of its unchangeable, hieratic character, canon law has tried to develop and make an adaptation to new needs. New causes of invalid marriages are being explored, and canonists endeavor to define them in legal language, as, for instance, incidents regarding homosexuality or psychopathic personality. Since, however, every human being contains at least some of the features which define these deviations from

1. *Op. cit.*, p. 291. On the same page, he quotes Walter Dirks: "Marriage used to be a social undertaking, and breaking away from it an individual affair; nowadays marriage has become an individual undertaking while adultery is a social and institutional affair. All resulting from the prevailing notion of autonomy" ("Was die Familie bedroht," in *Frankfurter Hefte* 6 (1951), p. 27).

the norm of human behavior, it will remain impossible to establish the exact limitations when homosexuality or a psychopathic personality, or similar such determinants of human behavior, lead to invalid marriages; and there seems to be only one solution to an impossibly complex problem, namely, the granting of divorce and the possibility of a new marriage.

It is not an exaggeration to say that the legislation of the Church ignores progress in psychology and psychiatry. Of course, behind every human act there is a "psychology" if we take the word in its everyday meaning. The great strides which psychology and psychiatry, together with psychoanalysis, have made in the twentieth century have still to find application in the law-creating activity of the Church—and this despite the fact that several Catholic universities in the United States have excellent schools of psychology or psychiatry.

When a Catholic reads of a civil divorce having been granted because of incompatibility he perhaps smiles sarcastically. There is no doubt that this incompatibility is very often lack of good will on the part of a spouse; however, it is equally true that there are numerous marriages in which there exist a real and unabridgeable incompatibility. Especially in our times of early marriages, partners to a marriage might be of so disparate backgrounds, devoid of any schooling in how to meet each other half way, that they are wholly incompatible psychologically. It will be of no use to advise them to have more understanding and patience of each other, because if they could do that they would not be so incompatible.

One could say that true incompatibility, as it results from deep-seated personality traits in concrete examples, constitutes a psychological impediment. Yet the law does not attend to it, chiefly because there never will be formed legal terms capable of defining it satisfactorily.[2]

2. Psychological incompatibility is a reality whose existence cannot be ignored: see R. J. McAllister, "Psychological Incompatibility," in *Marriage: A Psychological and Moral Approach.*

However, the fact that the subtleties of human nature cannot be fitted into the procrustean bed of legal language ought not to prevent the Church from supplementing this deficiency in single cases, and so apply the mercy of God to his suffering creatures.

The absolute prohibition of divorce and remarriage is quite often justified by the need of preserving as many families as possible and prevent their break-up. However, it can be said that this aim is rarely achieved. Actually, there seem to be few instances in which a Catholic couple in an unhappy marriage have recoiled from divorce because of the law of the Church. When the representatives of the Church come in contact with unhappy marriages, it is usually after the partners have separated, and very often when they have entered new non-Catholic or civil unions. It could be questioned whether it is desirable at all to compel such a couple to stay together merely because the law wishes it.

At the moment when partners to an unhappy marriage, Catholic or not, have resolved to separate, the idea of remarriage is usually completely absent from their mind. If anybody would suggest that they will be able to find a more congenial partner, they will vehemently disclaim any intention of ever joining their life with another man or woman. Their decision will hardly ever be influenced by the legal possibility of attaining divorce and remarriage.

Moreover, in practice Catholic families are not generally kept together by a consideration of the law. What the absolute prohibition of total divorce sometimes achieves is the prevention of a new marriage. But not even this is attained in a strict sense, since most couples disregard the law of the Church and enter civil or non-Catholic religious marriages. When they regret having violated the laws of the Church, it is then that the Church is called upon for help. Churchmen who suggest that the couple should either separate or promise a life of perpetual continence, show an unreal understanding of the reality of human nature.

96

Considering the well-being of the children alone, the question is not whether divorce has a bad influence upon their lives, but rather what effect the denial of a divorce and of a possible remarriage of the parents with more suitable partners will have. Most studies on this problem have come to the conclusion that the ending of a bad marriage is reflected in the children as a positive relief of psychological tensions, when the atmosphere of permanent menace of a break-up has been finally disposed of, and new patterns of personal relationships can be formed. Considering thus the interest of the children, divorce would seem preferable to the continuation of a seriously unhappy marriage; and remarriage at least of the parent who has the custody of the children to a more congenial partner will be a solution which will prove beneficial for the children in most cases.

Thus, what children of divorced parents have unfortunately lost, they could at least partially regain, if a stepfather or stepmother could extend to them all the facilities of a Catholic religious life, if they could with the newly acquired step-parent receive the sacraments, instead of being constantly reminded of the relative impropriety of the marital union of the parents.[3]

When organized society, for example the various nations, deny to their members the possibility of legal divorce entirely, or when they make divorce very difficult to obtain, they do this on the assumption that many marriages and families can be saved if the partners are compelled to continue life together. However, sociological studies, admittedly not too numerous as yet, have not confirmed this expectation. Morton H. Hunt has given some attention to this problem in his recent book *The*

---

3. In the decades between the two world wars Catholic parents all over the world were urged to accompany their children at the reception of First Holy Communion, flanking them at the communion rail. This has now been everywhere abandoned, and in a number of dioceses expressly forbidden, because of the heartache it caused to so many children when their parents had to refuse and were unable to explain the true reason why they could not receive the sacraments, namely, that they were living in unions not recognized by the Church.

World of the Formerly Married.[4] He admits that there is a period of adjustments in every marriage, but this refers solely to relatively superficial differences in the personalities of the spouses. There is much less likelihood that deep-seated personality differences and deficiencies could disappear by spontaneous remission.[5] Hunt has found that studies of case-workers and experts in family life regard spontaneous improvement of marriage conflicts extremely rare. Help from such outside agencies as marriage counselors or clergymen has been successful in a few instances in which the partners were sufficiently motivated. Even if marriage counseling and the pressure of social mores or religious laws should hold the partners together, this is far from conducive to a happy marriage. While divorce in such instances might not produce happiness either, the misery of feuding spouses forcing themselves to live together will be even more painful.

There is no doubt that divorce has a profound shattering effect upon the children. However, it is questionable whether the continuation of an unhappy family life of the parents is not even more the cause of permanent traumatic effects upon the children. The statistical association between divorce and delinquency does not have to be viewed as causative, but both might go back to a common origin, namely, to the actual causes for the total incompatibility of the parents.

Equally important in a consideration of the sociological context in which contemporary Catholics must work out their salvation is the witness of secular humanism.

4. Pp. 203ff.
5. "If the core personality is formed early and is quite unchangeable, it seems logical to conclude that personality is not appreciably changed by marriage. . . . Not only is the core personality established early but, once it is established, it tends henceforth to persist in a relatively enduring pattern. Within a not-too-flexible limit, it is the old story that the child is the father of the man" (J. R. Cavanagh, "Personality Development in Marriage," in *Marriage: A Psychological and Moral Approach*, p. 255).

98

The organization of God, the Church, and that of Caesar, the state, have never been able to achieve that harmony to which they are ideally destined. According to Catholic teaching of the last centuries, Church and state are both sovereign, each in its own province, and are obliged by divine will to cooperate for the welfare of men, who are members in both institutions.

It is still a widespread Catholic opinion that the civil government has an innate proclivity to be a foe of the Church. Much of this antagonism is the result of what Catholics view as the state's attempt to undermine that morality which the Church considers it her duty to defend. One obvious field of conflict concerns the regulation of the marriage relationship. The once strict laws of the Church are for all practical purposes superseded by the extreme permissiveness of civil law and its indulgent attitude towards divorce. Whatever, therefore, originates in the field of marriage law from the secular power is generally regarded as tainted and suspect, and there is a tendency, not without historical justification, to resist and reject all overtures from civil authority that bear on matters of sexuality.

However, in our opinion this attitude, although understandable, ought not be maintained without modification. Even if various nations have gone beyond what Catholics would regard as the limits of sound statesmanship with regard to divorce, it would be folly to deny that the men responsible for the government of nations as well as the teachers of civil law are just as eager to promote the common good and the advancement of morality as are the representatives of the Catholic Church and of Catholic theology.

It appears inadmissible, therefore, to assume that all the nations, and primitive societies, could be wrong and mistaken, or derelict in their duty of upholding sound principles of common and private good, especially as they affect marriage. This unanimity is not dissolved by the fact that at this time there still are a number of nations which have no provision for granting civil divorces to Catholics. It is common knowledge that this situation is maintained artificially by political pressure of Catholic parties. However, the preservation of such laws is against the ideal of freedom; and since they can usually be upheld only in a police state, the hour is not far off when this last remnant of the direct dominance of ecclesiastical power over civil law will be swept away.

While it cannot be denied that the secular power has not infrequently espoused dubious causes, to the men who decide the fate of secular society must be granted at least the quality of being witnesses to the general persuasion of mankind that the institution of marriage cannot be considered as functional without provision for some kind of divorce and remarriage. The continuous testimony of nations, governments, jurists, and even of all primitive societies, ought to be given a hearing in the court of Catholic theology.

The fact that all civilizations, states, and religious denominations today, while deploring the evil of divorce, permit its existence, except the Catholic Church alone, is in itself an invitation to re-study the entire problem from the standpoint of enlightened Catholic theology.

Marriage is said to be indissoluble according to the law of nature. But whose nature, and which nature? The figment or abstraction of theologians, or of the man as it appeared on this earth since the fall of Adam and Eve? Human nature is to be taken in its reality, with all its shortcomings, of course, variegated and differentiated in different individuals, but present in every man and woman. This is the true nature which human beings possess with the permission of the Creator, and only this concrete nature can be the basis for a system of rules, if the Maker of the universe is truly just.

The common good, which is said to be the justification for the prohibition of total divorce in marriage, is justified only, and exists solely, because it promotes the interests of the individual who falls under the law. It is distinguished from the individual good in that the latter benefits always the individual, while common good sometimes disregards the interests or benefits of some individuals, who are affected by measures taken for the welfare of the community, in order to secure ultimately certain advantages for a larger number of individuals.[6]

Serious reservations can be made against the way in which Catholic theologians employ the concept of common good in order to justify various legislative measures of the Church. There is often felt an absence of relationship with the merciful teaching of Christ. We therefore agree with John L. McKenzie when he says:

There are some reasons for doubting that the principle of law has a meaningful function in the Christian life. One who would wish to define the "common good" of the Church might find himself involved in impossible difficulties. The New Testament knows no other end of the Church than the incorporation of persons into Christ. The Church can have no accomplishment and no fulfillment which is not expressed in terms of individual persons. Renunciation is, of course, essentially involved in the Christian fulfillment; but Christian renunciation has this vitally important quality, that it is not Christian and salutary unless it is an entirely free choice of the person who renounces. The office of authority in the Church is to lead Christians to that renunciation which their faith demands of them, not to impose it. It cannot make personal decisions for its members. The supreme motive of the Christian moral act . . . is love; and the introduction of any type of pressure, even if it be no more than social pressure, attack the integrity of Christian love. Compulsion is alien to the genius of Christianity; and if there is a type of law which is not compulsive, no one has yet discovered it. Jesus did not remove the law of Judaism in order that it might be replaced by another law which would do the same thing.[7]

It is not contested that common good can impose great

6. "The Common Good as the supreme maxim of society, therefore, presupposes a higher and ultimate value: the human person. The Common Good is a real good only inasmuch as it results in the good of the individual. The Common Good derives its right to social supremacy from the fact that it is ordered in the final analysis to the end of man" (see D. J. Vella, "Canon Law and the Mystical Body," in *The Jurist*, p. 419).

7. "The Law in the New Testament," in *The Jurist*, p. 178.

sacrifice upon the subjects of the law. But there is, of course, included an essential justification for it: that the law thereby achieves its end, and that the sacrifice expected from the subjects is proportionate to the good attained for the benefit of more individuals. Thus the state can require subjects to submit even to the danger of death in war, in order to defend the very existence of the nation, but cannot impose that they sacrifice their lives solely to demonstrate an act of heroism to history.

However, when the law does not attain its proposed goals for a larger number of individuals, because of external circumstances,[8] then it can be said that it does not promote any more the common good and that its existence becomes thereby unjustified. As we have seen, this can be asserted to a certain degree of the denial to separated Catholics of remarriage with other marriage partners. Close observation in a number of countries of Europe and America will compel one to conclude that in the present situation the number of individuals, spouses and children, that incur sufferings because of the impossibility of remarriage is considerably greater than that of those who might benefit from the present law.[9]

While in all societies, even the most primitive ones, and including those which permit polygamy and group marriage, marriage is always regarded as a permanent, life-long union, all civilizations, nations, and religions have permitted divorce and remarriage, except the Western Catholic or Roman Church in the last millennium. These groups of organized humanity were well aware of the importance for the good of society that marriage should be stable and enduring. It was not due to lack of moral fiber that they permitted divorce and remarriage in

8. "In all questions of family morality it can be expected with a fairly high degree of certainty that 90 per cent or more of the population will gradually adapt themselves to the general opinoin if this is spread by newspapers, magazines, films, radio and television and remains uncontradicted" (Häring, op. cit., p. 58).

9. "Laws, even the natural law, are for men, not men for laws. Thus the conclusions of many theologians need to be re-thought" (Francis Simons, S.V.D., bishop of Indore, India, during the third session of the Second Vatican Council, October, 1965).

certain instances, but rather out of the reflection that too rigid a law might render true the ancient adage, *Summum ius, summa iniuria* (Right pushed to the extreme is extreme wrong). It is only the theologians of the Catholic Church who contradict this general social experience, both because they sincerely believe they are confronted by a divine prohibition, and because they often do not exercise the freedom which is rightly theirs—a matter we will take up shortly. Even the Church applies her strictness in refusing the permission of remarriage only to one sole class of marriages, though the most numerous, while readily granting divorces to the other kinds.[10]

It cannot be denied that the granting of complete divorces will lead to inequities. However, there is no law, and no human action, which has not to permit also some undesirable marginal sequels. This is due to the limited capacity of human intellects and corrupted human wills. All lawgivers are aware of it.

10. One may wonder how much the doctrine of absolute indissolubility is influenced by the fact that its promoters and formulators are celibate secular and regular priests. Noonan has advanced the same thought with respect to the problem of contraception: "In declaring evil an act of contraception performed lawfully by wedded persons, the theologians had condemned an act which was literally beyond their experience . . . Obviously, experience is not a precondition for judging the morality of an act intelligently. All condemn murder, though few are murderers. Observation, empathy with the experience of others, reasoning, can be the process of moral judgment. At the same time the characteristic problems and joys of one occupation or state of life are usually more acutely perceived and feelingly expressed by those who experience them. To judge rightly the morality of particular acts may require close listening to those who have had experience of the way of living in which the questions arise" (*Contraception*, p. 488).

At the Second Vatican Council, Patriarch Maximos IV coined the phrase "bachelor psychosis."

V. J. Dunigan opposes remonstrations of the laity that their specific interests are not adequately represented by celibate clergymen with the counterargument that a judge is capable of convicting a murderer although he himself has not murdered anyone ("Birth Control and Politics," in *The Priest*). However, his example is precisely a proof against his own thesis, for in fact, judges are not permitted to condemn anyone for murder. The law has placed this responsibility into the hands of the legal laity, namely, the twelve members of the jury, the peers of the murderer.

103

The only remedy is to adapt the law to the changed situations and needs as quickly as possible, in proportion to the importance of the law within the legal system, and the good it is supposed to protect. There are two possibilities in this aspect: speedy adaptation of the law, either by new enactments of the legislator or by restrictive or extenuating interpretation by the judiciary, or inflexible enforcement of a rigid principle, irrespective of how many individuals will suffer from such an application.

3. NO PROTEST?

In order to support the traditional denial of divorce, use is sometimes made also of the argument that the Catholic Church has never experienced a protest against the rigidity of her position in this matter. Apart from the fact that this is simply not true, we must point out that the Catholic Church is not an organization which encourages free exchange of opinions, but rather unconsciously represses any attempt at protest with all the power of her legal system and bureaucratic apparatus.[1] There can be no doubt that in some instances the Church has been right to employ such means against scurrilous attacks whether from the outside or the inside. It is unavoidable in an organization composed of human beings that mistakes will be made, even though the present spirit of *aggiornamento* is supposed to introduce a more equitable treatment for dissenters.[2]

1. See Rahner, *op. cit.*, on the limits in discussing questions that conflict with the teaching of the Church: ". . . there is always a strong tendency to narrow down far too closely the range of what parts of the Faith can be legitimately discussed" (p. 27).
2. P. Pinxten, referring to the problem of contraception, disputes the claim that it is an infallibly established doctrine. His reasoning is at least partially valid with respect to divorce as well: ". . . one can hardly speak of 'consensus' when a truly open discussion between theologians and other specialists in the field has never taken place, when the opinion of the bishops on this matter has never been requested, and when there has never been question of consulting the most inter-

With the present ecclesiastical censorship, there is not much possibility of advancing new ideas if they oppose long-held beliefs, unless perhaps if the author has gained international prominence or is a member of the hierarchy. The remarks of Archbishop Elias Zoghby at the Second Vatican Council are an example. The reaction outside the Council was instantaneous and it was necessary to hold a special press conference the following day at which the Archbishop had to offer an explanatory comment. Of course, the spontaneity of the reaction was in direct proportion to the urgency of a solution to this burning problem, and it was realized as such by the entire world. It is rightly felt that if divorce is simply mentioned as the last solution for extreme spiritual suffering by millions of Catholics, then this in itself constitutes an advocacy and implies a promotion of divorce and the break-up of marriages. Had it not been for the new spirit pervading the Church, the matter of divorce would perhaps not even have been broached.

Another member of the hierarchy whose voice was recently heard in favor of divorce and remarriage is F. Simons, who rightly remarks: "Jesus told the scribes that Moses had allowed divorce and remarriage because of the hardness of his people's hearts, but do we not also have today a number of people who find it impossible to make a success of a marriage, or to live a continent life once their marriage has broken up?" [3]

The absence of current statements favoring the concession of total divorce cannot be construed as meaning that the Church is faced with a newly instigated movement, aiming at the de-

_____

ested people—married laymen. In view of the byzantinism from which ecclesiastical circles have suffered during recent decades more than ever before—and from which we begin to be freed by Pope John's and the Council's attitude—one must not be surprised that 'the doubt which exists in large circles' only now begins to break out. It is, in my opinion, typical that this doubt after so many years of repression has already spread so rapidly and so widely. Consequently, on the basis of this criterion one can certainly not claim infallibility for the present doctrine" (quoted in L. Dupré, *Contraception and Catholics,* p. 32).

3. "The Catholic Church and the New Morality," in *Cross Currents,* p. 443.

struction of the moral and legal order. Of course, non-Catholics and members of the Church who have defected have remonstrated. However, what was felt, thought, and said by faithful sons of the Church, to whom obedience to the ecclesiastical authorities was of paramount importance, ought primarily to be considered here. If only a few dared or have been able to let their voice be heard, we should not draw the conclusion that many others do not recognize the needs of the Church; rather, we should ascribe this silence to misplaced loyalty and to the pressures of the militant, uncompromising, and inflexible character of authority in the Church.

As we have seen, most Catholic authors, writing on the subject of indissolubility and divorce in the past, give the impression that only a few of the Fathers were vacillating on this point, that the Western Church suffered only sporadic instances of relapse into "laxity," and that after the first millennium there was everywhere established the principle of absolute indissolubility.

But the witness of history is different. In respect to the first ten centuries, the reader can examine for himself the original texts of Fathers, synods, and popes found in the appendixes to this book. For the centuries following the great reform of Cluny, one can state that the theory taught at the newly established universities was clear and apodictic, and excluded any kind of divorce. But the practice was often diametrically opposed to theory, and since the teaching was in fact only leniently urged, no true opposition was engendered. Following are a few such testimonies.[4]

The Council of Bourges (1031) refused to recognize the right of remarriage to those who dismissed a spouse on grounds other than adultery (*sine culpa fornicationis*). Thus, had adultery been charged and proved, divorce and remarriage would have been permitted.

4. See J. Dauvillier, *Le mariage dans le droit classique de l'Eglise depuis le Décret de Gratien (1140) jusqu'à la mort de Clément V (1314)*, pp. 280–289.

The Synod of Tours (1060) exacted the punishment of excommunication for those who repudiated their wives without the intervention of the Church (*sine judicio Ecclesiae*)—which obviously meant that a new marriage could be permitted by the Church.

A husband in a consummated marriage is reported as having gotten the approval of Innocent III (1198–1216) to receive holy orders after his wife had agreed to the separation on the condition that she could remarry.

According to a law applied in the court of the Latin Kingdom of Jerusalem (between 1173 and 1187), a marriage could be dissolved and the husband could remarry if the wife had incurred leprosy or some other grave disability, and on the condition that she entered the religious life.

From a decretal of Pope Lucius III (1181–1185), it is known that those Crusaders who were taken captive by the Saracens considered themselves entitled to remarry.

In Ireland, total divorces were granted up to the fourteenth century, when finally the ecclesiastical norms prevailed.

The Greek matrimonial courts of Cyprus, under the supervision of the Latin-rite Archbishop, granted total divorce even in the fourteenth century.[5]

Similarly in other parts of Western Europe there was a great leniency in the application of the teaching of the Church.[6]

Another reason why the absence of the legal institution of divorce was for centuries not found obnoxious was the ease with which marriages were annulled.[7] This does not have to be explained by intentional relaxation or circumvention of the law, but rather by the fact that certain grounds for nullity are even today not yet theoretically clear and fully developed.

Also, the rise and rapid spread of Protestantism, of which one of the conspicuous tenets was the possibility of divorce, can

5. Zhishman, *op. cit.*, p. 115.
6. E. Esmein, *Le mariage en droit canonique,* vol. II, p. 81.
7. A. Marongin, "Divorzio (storia)," in *Enciclopedia del Diritto,* vol. XIII, p. 493, quoting Tamassia, *La famiglia italiana nei secoli decimoquarto e decimosesto* (Milan-Palermo, 1910).

be considered in part a protest in the matter of divorce. In the subsequent polemic, doubt was raised whether Catholic theology was justified in its restrictive interpretation of the passages of the New Testament referring to divorce. In addition to Erasmus of Rotterdam, who was suspected of Protestant leanings, two other Catholic theologians of unquestioned orthodoxy may be mentioned, Cardinal Cajetan and Ambrose Catharinus.

Cardinal Thomas Cajetan, O.P. (1469–1534), was the representative of several popes in the struggle against Luther and Protestantism, and he is still esteemed as one of the foremost exponents of the Thomistic school. This renowned writer, whom Pope Clement VII called a "lamp of the Church," expressed in his commentary on St. Paul [8] the opinion that the clause in Matthew 19, 9, "except because of fornification," ought to be understood as granting total divorce. He compares the regulations of Jesus with that of Paul in respect to marriages with non-baptized persons. Both are from God, but while Jesus' is clear and determined, Paul's appears clouded. Christ assigns freedom of separation only to the husband, while Paul grants it to both spouses. Cajetan was bewildered and could see no justifying scriptural reason why Paul's concession should be so broadly interpreted as allowing total divorce, while what Jesus expressly permitted should be interpreted as allowing nothing more than simple separation from cohabitation. His objection was not directed against the explanation given by Catholic theologians of Paul's concession, but against the narrow understanding of the meaning of Jesus' word.

He repeated his opinion in his commentary on Matthew 19:

. . . because I do not dare to put myself against the torrent of teachers and ecclesiastical judges, I said therefore that the text [Mt. 19] decides nothing concerning the dismissal of the woman fornicator. However, I understand from this law of Our Lord Jesus Christ that it is permitted to a Christian man to dismiss a wife because of carnal fornication on the part of his wife, and that he

8. *Epistolae Pauli et aliorum apostolorum ad graecam veritatem castigatae . . . iuxta sensum litteralem enarratae,* pp. 123 *verso* and 125 *recto.*

can take another wife, excepting of course a [contrary] definition from the Church which has not yet appeared.[9]

Cajetan compares the permission granted by Paul to divorce a marriage (1 Cor. 7, 15) with that allowed by Jesus (Mt. 19, 9). He cannot understand how Paul could permit more than Christ, and implies that if we accept the broad interpretation of the Pauline Privilege, we ought to interpret Jesus' concession at least equally generously.

Bishop Ambrose Catharinus, O.P. (+ 1553), a contemporary of Cardinal Cajetan and an extraordinary but erratic genius, bitterly assailed Cajetan for certain opinions expressed by the latter in his biblical studies. Yet Catharinus too voiced objections against the narrow interpretation of the regulations on divorce in the New Testament:

Neither from the Gospel nor from the Apostle can it be deduced that it is not permitted to contract another marriage because of adultery. (It is, however, forbidden by various canons of the Church, which could not have been decreed except in virtue of the decision and authority of the Church.) But this is permitted to the husband alone, not to the wife, in such a way that the bond is dissolved in relation to the husband because of the adultery of the wife, but it is not dissolved in relation to the wife, who is obliged to remain without hope of a second marriage.[10]

There are other protests, perhaps sporadic and insignificant. But that they occurred at all—not their statistical frequency—is the surprising factor. In the three centuries following the Council of Trent around thirty books were published by Catholics denying that the indissolubility of marriage was an infallible doctrine of the Church. Most of these authors advanced

9. It is significant that Perrone, Rokosvany, and other Catholic defenders of indissolubility omit from their quotations of Cajetan (*ibid.*, fol. 44 a-b) the last part: " . . . because the papal decrees in this matter are not defining faith but concern judicial facts. The popes themselves confess . . . that the Roman pontiffs have sometimes erred in their solutions of marriage problems" ("Profitentur autem ipsimet pontifices . . . Romanos pontifices in his judiciis matrimoniorum errasse"). See F. von Gunten. "La doctrine de Cajetan sur l'indissolubilité du mariage," in *Angelicum*.

10. *Adnotationes in commentaria Caietani*, p. 500.

in their works other, certainly non-Catholic and heretical teachings, and as could be expected, their obnoxious doctrines were rejected *en bloc* with less reprehensible suggestions.

One could apply to this entire situation what John T. Noonan has said in respect to the discussion of the permissibility of contraception:

Administrative control of theological speculation produced a situation in which one could pretend that what was written represented what was taught by all theologians. The result was not insincerity on the part of those who wrote openly with a strong conviction of the rightness of their views, but silence, involuntary or voluntary, from those who disagreed. An unhealthy climate for discussion was created when it was not certain that all the thinking of theologians was being communicated . . .[11]

Nor did the Catholic Oriental Church, though too weak to resist, readily accept the principles of the Roman Church in this regard. Among the Greeks in Italy and in the Venetian possessions the granting of divorces compelled Clement VIII (1592–1605) to instruct the Latin-rite bishops, to whom these Greek rite Catholics were subject, not to permit nor even tolerate this custom. Patriarch Sergius of the Maronite Church, which was in its entirety united with the Catholic Church since the thirteenth century under Innocent III, had to forbid divorce because of adultery and disease as late as 1596; and the Maronite Synod of 1736 had explicitly to forbid the granting of divorce because of an absence of seven years by one spouse. The group which continued the longest in granting divorces on the ground of adultery and malicious desertion were the Catholic Romanians of the Byzantine rite. As late as in 1858 it was necessary for Pius IX to insist in an instruction to the Romanian bishops that the practice of the Roman Church on divorce be accepted.[12]

Another kind of remonstrance was made by individual

11. *Contraception*, p. 485.
12. *Collectanea S. Congregationis de Propaganda Fide seu Decreta, Instructiones, Rescripta, pro apostolicis missionibus*, 1154. See also the instructions of the Holy Office to the Oriental bishops in 1883 (*ibid.*, 1588) and in 1890 (*ibid.*, 1740).

priests, as in Austria, who disregarded the censures of the Church against them, suspension and excommunication, and for years blessed arbitrarily the new marriages of divorced Catholics. The movement of the Old Catholics in several countries of Europe gained many of its followers because of its willingness to permit remarriages.

A real contribution to the solution of this problem in our own time will come from those theologians who are able to show Catholic theology a way out from its present dead-end by offering new avenues of approach. Such an attempt has been made by William R. O'Connor and A. Bride. We shall reconsider O'Connor's suggestions in our concluding chapter, but Bride's may be briefly looked at now. He suggests that the Church modify the concept of sacramentality and of consummation in marriage to such a degree that marriages could easily be recognized as invalid and non-existent, and dissolved as such. In respect to one small group of marriages, the sterile ones, in which there is a clearly established absolute and permanent impossibility of offspring—excluding thereby the marriages of the old—he proposed to have them declared dissoluble since they totally preclude the realization of one of the primary purposes of marriage, the procreation of children.[13] The possibility of a divine authority existing within the Church to dissolve even sacramental, consummated marriages was recognized also by L. Bender: "It seems to me that we cannot deny that God can dissolve also a ratified and consummated marriage and that he can grant the power to the Supreme Pontiff." [14]

4. INADEQUATE SOLUTIONS

The agonizing problem of millions of Catholics who are living in second marriages without the blessing of the Church has

13. A. Bride, "Le pouvoir du Souverain Pontife sur le mariage des infidèles," in Revue de Droit Canonique, p. 98 f.
14. De Matrimonio, p. 722.

brought forward various proposals by Catholic theologians earn-estly seeking—by tortuously devious means—to resolve the im-passe without violating the principle of absolute indissolubility of sacramental marriages. Their proposals can be viewed as attempts to unravel the Gordian knot when a blow from the sword seems the only remedy. But to understand their pro-posals, it will first be necessary to define some technical terms.

In the first place, marriage is a contract even when it is the sacramental union of the baptized persons. It is a contract of a special kind, but there are certain essential features—among others—of every contract which are also part of the marriage contract:

(1) No true contract can be established except by the free consent of the contrahents, in the case of marriage, of a man and woman who are free and capable of entering into the state of matrimony. This consent cannot be supplied by any power outside the contrahents.

(2) Every contract contains certain conditions to which the contrahents mutually oblige themselves. The conditions which belong to the nature or essence of the marriage contract are outside the bargaining power of the contrahents, and are deter-mined in advance for each and every marriage by law, whether natural, ecclesiastical, or civil.

(3) It is also in the nature of a contract that the will to fulfill the obligations which were freely agreed upon exists not only at the moment when the contract is concluded, but that it continues to exist during the duration of the contract. If a contrahent refuses to comply with the conditions of the con-tract, he not only gives the partner the right of reciprocity, that is, frees him of the corresponding obligation, but he might prepare the way to a dissolution of the contract.

(4) The refusal to comply with essential conditions of the contract either dissolves the contract automatically, or gives the right to rescind it. This is in the nature of every contract, and this is also recognized by the Church in respect to marriage, at

least partially, when she permits the perpetual separation of the spouses from matrimonial cohabitation.

Now the suggestion has been made that the Church could change the conditions of the contract of marriage in such a way as to facilitate a later annulment because of the invalidity of the contract. It was pointed out how the Church had freely made modifications in the marriage form whereby, for example, a marriage is invalid if it was celebrated by Oriental Catholics before an Orthodox priest on January 21, 1965, but valid if this was done the next day, January 22, 1965.[1] Let us thus set up such conditions for the marriage contract which can then be invoked as a source of invalidity and lead to easier annulments. Those who propose such devious escapes from a difficult situation as a replacement for a straightforward dissolution of marriage, do no present any ideas how this could actually be done. They also ignore the fact that the Church would perhaps help some marriages but in doing so would render as many marriages invalid, in which the spouses wish to stay together in valid sacramental bonds.

Another speculative suggestion proposes to study the possibility of whether a marriage between two baptized persons could not be a simple natural marriage. According to the teaching of the Catholic Church, every valid marriage between two persons who have been baptized is automatically a sacramental union, independently of the intention of the contrahents. But should two baptized persons by a positive act of the will decide to enter into a non-sacramental marriage, this marital union would be no marriage at all, because an essential part of marriage between baptized persons was excluded.

However, natural marriage and baptism can be joined in *one* person, as, for example, when with papal dispensation a Catholic marries an unbaptized person in a Catholic Church. According to the majority of theologians, such a marriage is not a sacrament because the unbaptized partner cannot be a

1. See the *Decree on Eastern Catholic Churches,* art. 18, and Pospishil, *Orientalium Ecclesiarum,* pp. 44–54.

recipient of it, and since the marriage bond or contract is indivisible, neither can the Catholic partner receive the sacramental grace.[2] Thus, a baptized person, Catholic or non-Catholic, can be validly married in a non-sacramental bond of marriage, which bond is capable of being dissolved by the Church in virtue of the so-called Petrine Privilege. Why, then, should this not be extended to the case of *two* baptized persons? Two possibilities are conceivable: (1) Two baptized persons, in this case two Catholics, could be permitted to contract a natural, non-sacramental marriage. They would have the choice either to enter a sacramental, indissoluble marriage, or a natural, non-sacramental marriage, which could be dissolved by the Church, but which nevertheless would be a sacred and religious bond. Present Catholic teaching excludes this,[3] but the Ethiopian Coptic Church (non-Catholic), for instance, is said to have given her faithful this possibility. Thus partners enter marriage in their younger years quite informally and such unions can be dissolved by divorce. Only in later years, at an advanced age, do they request the blessing of the Church, after which the marriage is considered sacramental and indissoluble.

(2) Another possibility would be to assume that the sacramental character could cease to exist in a marital union of Christians. According to Catholic teaching, the sacrament follows the contract in marriage. This principle is especially evident in a marriage of a baptized and an unbaptized person, which is a natural, non-sacramental bond. If the unbaptized partner then receives baptism, this marriage becomes automatically a sacramental one, even if the partners have already

2. C. A. Schleck, *The Sacrament of Matrimony. A Dogmatic Study,* pp. 104 ff.

3. Instruction of the Holy Office, of July 6, 1817. Benedict XIV did not wish to decide whether there could be a valid non-sacramental marriage between Christians (Constitution *Redditae,* 1746. See W. M. Plöchl, *Geschichte des Kirchenrechts,* vol. IV, pp. 194, 200).

dissolved their union, perhaps by obtaining a civil divorce decree. It is a paradox of Catholic theology that an actually *non-existing* marriage can thereby automatically become a sacrament in spite of the fact that the spouses have severed their marital union by a divorce decree, and have married other partners. This automatic and compulsory sacramentalization shall be illustrated by some frequently occurring examples.

(1) John, who is unbaptized, marries Kathleen, a baptized Lutheran. After three years of marriage they separate and obtain a divorce decree. John now marries Emily, a baptized Presbyterian, while Kathleen marries David, a baptized Methodist. At this point, according to the teaching of the Catholic Church, the marriages John-Emily and Kathleen-David are invalid, because the marriage John-Kathleen can be dissolved only by the pope as a natural, non-sacramental marriage. Under the influence of Emily, John joins her Church and receives baptism. Now his marriage with Kathleen has become a sacramental union, although an unconsummated one.

(2) Peter professed Protestantism as a son of Baptist parents but he neglected to receive baptism as an adult. He married Charlotte, a Jewess. After a marriage of three years they separate and Peter marries Mary, a devout Protestant, under whose influence he receives baptism in her Church. Charlotte meets Donald, a Lutheran, receives baptism in that denomination, and marries him. After his death in an automobile accident she wishes to marry Francis, a Catholic. Before she can do this, she has to receive a dispensative dissolution of her marriage to Peter as a sacramental, non-consummated marriage. Why?

The marriage Peter-Charlotte was originally a natural, non-sacramental marriage. Such a marriage, although it does not concern Catholics, can be dissolved, according to Catholic doctrine, by the Privilege of St. Paul. The nature of this marriage was not changed by the baptism of Peter, because Charlotte was then still unbaptized. However, when she was baptized in

115

the Lutheran Church her marriage to Peter became a marital union of two baptized persons and automatically also a sacrament, and this legal effect takes place although there is no semblance whatever of a contractual relationship, the essence of any marriage. They had separated from each other by a divorce, knew nothing of each other's whereabouts, were not aware of the Catholic doctrine on marriage, but still miraculously and automatically their non-existing union became a sacrament. Sacramental marriages are indissoluble only if they were not sexually consummated. Since Peter and Charlotte had not seen each other for years, they could not have had intercourse, and the pope could then grant a dispensative dissolution.

Although these legal fictions can all be justified—and are—as straight deductions from higher principles, it seems rather absurd that the sacred character of a sacrament should be so forcefully, artificially, and extraneously imposed upon an actually non-existing relationship.

A third approach to make possible the dissolution of Catholic marriages which have already dissolved is to search out new reasons for nullity. A justified suspicion can be entertained that marriages which have foundered, perhaps quickly, did so because there were from the very outset causes which rendered them humanly impossible, and thereby also in a certain sense null.

The field in which reinforcements for this proposal may be found is psychiatry. Psychiatry as the determinant of possible grounds for declaring marriage invalid has long been accepted by canon law since insanity in its various degrees and forms is recognized as a factor potentially influencing consent to such a degree that it is not a free act of the will. The last decades have seen a progressive acceptance of psychiatric evidence in trials before ecclesiastical marriage tribunals. However, this evidence must refer solely to forms of insanity—although it is now admitted that impairment of the intellect alone is not sufficient if the emotional concomitants of a human act are abnormal, that is, when, even though intellectual faculties are not impaired, the individual nevertheless uses them in an abnormal way.

Finally, in an effort to solve the problem one might propose a new definition of the concept of consummation of marriage. At the present time, only the physical, sexual union is taken into consideration, and a marriage can be declared null or dissolved by a papal dispensation only if no bodily intercourse has taken place. However, perhaps the concept of consummation ought to be expanded to include spiritual union also. If it can be reasonably proved that a spiritual union did not exist from the beginning, or ever, then the Church should be able to declare a marriage under consideration null and void.

But though there might be a possibility of defining the meaning of spiritual union, how can one draw the exact line of demarcation as to when and if the spiritual union of spouses was achieved? Canon law employs in its distinction between valid and invalid marriages the principle of total presence or absence of some requirement. Either there was insanity, or impotence, or an invalidating impediment, or there was not. As we noted above, no attention can be paid to the quantity or degree of a condition. Even when a marriage is impugned as invalid because of grave fear, it is assumed that grave and light fear differ not in degree, but in kind. For such reasons, it seems impossible to delineate the condition of validity satisfactorily to a point which would enable the ecclesiastical judge to apply it to marriage failures.

In the present system of canon law one cannot conclude from the fact of the breakdown of a marriage that the spiritual union of full "consummation" had never been achieved. The condition of spiritual union would have to be determined in such a way that its presence or absence could objectively be established in every marriage, independently of the partners' wish to dissolve it or not. Since this seems to be impossible, it is difficult to see how this proposal can lead to a solution of the divorce-remarriage problem.

117

5. TOLERANCE THROUGH DISSIMULATION

It is well known how often it is impossible canonically to prove the invalidity of a marriage although the representatives of the Church, the personnel of the ecclesiastical tribunal, might be personally convinced of it. The facts as told by an unsophisticated person may remove any doubt in the mind of the listening official, but he has to reject the plea if the witnesses or documents so essential to a legal proceeding cannot be produced. Sometimes evidence cannot be furnished only because of political conditions such as those which have taken place in Eastern Europe, and which prevent efficient communication with persons living behind the iron curtain. What heartbreak is then felt if a servant of the Church must refuse his help only because the legalistic rules of a bureaucratic process cannot be satisfied.

In other instances there is the problem to be faced of judging the innermost thoughts, ideas, and intentions of a person on the occasion of his marriage. The law is justifiably reluctant to accept only the word of the parties interested concerning what their mental state was at that time. One does not have to assume fraud and collusion, but it is evident that recollections of past events are colored by present needs and desires. The tribunal does not want to take a risk and will thus reject an affirmative decision that would be based solely on the deposition of the interested parties; and if they have nothing else to offer in evidence their request for an annulment must be refused.

It must be obvious, then, that the legal requirements will never be able to do justice to the spiritual needs of the members of the Church. Moral theology is entirely different in this respect because it can grant priority to the conscience of each individual and reduce imputability for all actions to the level of direct communication between creature and Creator. Everyone is judged by God according to the objective norms of divine law—but always according to one's personal intellectual

118

understanding of the law. In addition, all individual determinants of one's acts, as physiological and psychological inclinations, temptations resulting from the circumstances, and so forth, are taken into consideration with a degree of perfect, infallible accuracy that is utterly unattainable by any human judicial institution.

The question is whether this realization of how imperfect are the means capable of detecting the invalidity of marriages and of proving it judicially, could not be used to inaugurate a more tolerant attitude by the Church towards Catholics who have remarried after a civil divorce. Could not such Catholics be admitted to the sacraments, under the assumption that perhaps their marriages too are valid because of some general, canonical, undefinable ground of invalidity in respect to the first marriages? How otherwise can one explain the apparent wholesomeness of the second marriage: spouses in perfect harmony and love, children raised according to the laws of God and the Church, exemplary compliance with all demands of the Church, unless one assumes that the second marriage possesses the true essence of a good marriage—and this because the first one lacked some essential ingredient to make a true marriage according to the plan of God? The invalidity of the first marriage might not be determinable according to the man-made regulations of the Church; and therefore the inability of the legal system to satisfy what is right and just ought to be supplemented by a tolerant attitude towards such remarried members of the Church.

These and similar ideas are now being circulated in many countries. Robert Adolfs, O.S.A., reports in his article "The Tragedy of Broken Marriages," [1] under the subtitle "A Gentler Practice,"

Fortunately, a much milder pastoral practice has been applied in recent years, in many dioceses. When it is definitely established that the first marriage bond has been completely severed, the local pastor may allow those married in a civil ceremony to receive

1. In *Jubilee,* pp. 46–48.

sacraments in private. If the non-religious marriage of the pair in question is not known in the parish they can even receive the sacraments in public. In any case, all cause of scandal must be eliminated. In so doing, the basic consideration is that, whereas the law of the Church is powerless, the pastoral, entirely spiritual care of the faithful can go much farther. Much here depends on the insight and wisdom of the local pastor. Officially, of course, such pastoral practice cannot be sanctioned and pastors who urge the strict application of Church laws cannot be blamed.

Yet it must be evident to everyone that the present situation is most unsatisfactory. There is too much tension between ecclesiastical law and pastoral practice. Not only the married couple in question, but also many a parish priest, is confronted with a troubled conscience. As I see it, the present laws of marriage in the Latin Church are no longer adequate for the marriage problems of today.

If this should hold true for some parts of Europe, especially the Netherlands where Father Adolfs lives, no such practice is known to exist at the present time in the United States or in Canada, although similar ideas are being advanced privately.

C. van der Poel, C.S.Sp., professor of moral theology and canon law at St. Mary's Seminary in Norwalk, Connecticut, has published, in collaboration with B. Peters and T. Beemer, professors of moral theology at Warmond, Netherlands, an article titled "Co-Habitation in 'Marital State of Mind.' " [2] The authors come to the conclusion that:

It cannot be *unqualifiedly* maintained that *concubinarii* are excluded in principle from receiving the sacraments. We are convinced that there can be very real circumstances because of which *certain* persons who live in such a co-habitation in a marital state of mind can be morally justified before God and before the Church because they *cannot* live in any other way, because of the imperfection in which a man of good will sometimes *must* live.

Let it be said explicitly that no well-determined and concrete rules can be drawn up for this practice. In judging a co-habitation "in marital state of mind" much room must be given to the

2. *Art. cit.,* pp. 566–577.

120

individual pastor in his conversation with the faithful who live in such circumstances. However, in these pages we have tried to present some criteria which are, at least in our opinion, of fundamental importance in forming a judgment.

But it can be doubted that such considerations will ever lead to the formulation of a theory which could be applied safely in practice. Häring is correct when he sees such a kind of forbearance excluded by higher principles: "Moral-pedagogical temporary toleration (by silence and inaction) is excluded by the New Testament order for mankind under the law of Christ." [3] At best, such tolerance is only a palliative which the great majority of Catholics affected will not be able to make use of. The inherent inconsistencies and the lack of logic of these and similar suggestions is a sign of the despair to which conscientious shepherds of souls are driven when they are confronted with the plight of so many divorced and remarried Catholics.[4] In other words, the Church must make use of her authority.

6. TOWARDS THE SOLUTION

If it is true that the Church possesses no power to dissolve a sacramental marriage, then this should not permit any exception, for whatever reason. Actually, there is one exception, namely, the dispensative dissolution of sexually non-consummated marriages by the Pope. There is also the dissolution of such a marriage in virtue of perpetual profession taken in a religious order with solemn profession, that is, when one or both spouses in a non-consummated marriage enter an order and then take final solemn vows. We do not refer specifically to this

3. *Op. cit.,* p. 266.
4. Joseph T. Nolan, in his review of the article "Co-Habitation in 'Marital State of Mind'" by van der Poel-Peters-Beemer, while sympathetic to the thesis presented, cannot help pointing out the internal contradictions which are inevitable in any attempt to preserve the principle of absolute indissolubility and at the same time to tolerate the existence of invalid marriages.

latter possibility because such instances are rare and belong largely in the realm of mere speculation. To this it is to be added that no married person can validly enter a religious institute without a papal dispensation. So, in the final analysis, it is always the pope who has to intervene in the dissolution of non-consummated marriages.

But as we have seen, consummation alone does not suffice to render a marriage indissoluble, because then the Church could not dissolve natural, non-sacramental marriages after they were consummated sexually. Neither is the sacramental character alone enough to explain indissolubility, because then the Church could not dissolve non-consummated sacramental marriages. There is also no adequate explanation why the jointure of sacramental character and the fact of consummation should make marriage indissoluble. Since it cannot be denied that the dissolution by papal "dispensation" involves a valid, Christian, sacramental marriage, which is supposed to be indissoluble, though not consummated, theologians have difficulty in justifying such a practice on theoretical grounds. They can only point to the fact that the Roman pontiff has granted such dispensations since the Middle Ages, and that it cannot be presumed that he would act against a law of God. We accept this argumentation wholeheartedly and believe that the Church cannot be wrong in exercising such authority; moreover, we believe the Church possesses also the same authority in respect to any and all marriages, Christian, sacramental, or natural. The fact that sexual integrity is still preserved in the woman cannot be the reason for this exception, because it applies also to widows and also to cases when the parties even produced children but then had no intercourse after the marriage rite itself.

A marriage is not consummated when no real intercourse has taken place. Intercourse in the legal meaning is to be understood as the penetration of the female organ by the male copulative organ, and the deposition of semen therein. There are two contingencies when such failure of consummation can

122

occur: (1) Organic or psychological difficulties can make it impossible for a couple to have normal intercourse. Organic deficiencies, as the absence of essential parts of the genitalia, are rather rarely encountered, but psychological difficulties are a frequent occurrence. They can prevent the man from having an erection sufficient to permit penetration of the female organ, or can induce in the woman a spasm of the muscle at the orifice of the vagina which prevents entrance of the male organ.

Psychological difficulties are experienced at the beginning of many marriages, but they usually disappear sooner or later. However, when they persist they make life quite miserable to the spouses, especially because of sexual union's involvement of their entire personalities. According to modern authorities, such conditions cannot usually be removed by any means, though the Code of Justinian permitted separation of the spouses after an unsuccessful trial period of three years. Generally, they separate and divorce much earlier.

The psychological difficulty is as a rule not permanent, and usually exists solely in respect to the other spouse. It can disappear when the partner meets a more congenial and understanding partner. The normal case which the canonist encounters in his practice is that of the husband who cannot perform his marital duties because of a psychological block. The Church in then asked for relief to permit the other spouse to enter another marriage. The consequent dissolution is then often advantageous to the man too, for he may subsequently meet a woman with whom he is not sexually incapacitated.

One should add that only the inability to consummate marriage from the very beginning is taken into consideration by canon law. If it developed or appeared at a later period, after the spouses had had complete intercourse, it is not considered at all, and does not come under this heading. There are known instances when normal intercourse with penetration of the female organ had never taken place—although children were born from the union—because the semen had been deposited

123

only at the entrance of the vagina. This would not constitute consummation of marriage, just as artificial insemination does not. A marriage would remain unconsummated also if coitus were undertaken in such a way that the sperm was intentionally not deposited in the female organ, either because the semination took place outside the vagina or contact of the sperm with the vagina was prevented by mechanical means.[1] For a number of prudent reasons, the Holy See is reluctant to accept petitions for a dissolution of marriage in which the only grounds offered are those above, even if it should be possible to prove that not even one true consummative intercourse, as presently defined, had ever taken place.[2]

(2) Another way that a marriage can remain non-consummated has nothing to do with sexual abuse or indeficiencies. In some exceptional instances persons enter marriages in circumstances where cohabitation is impossible after the marriage ceremony, even though they might have lived in a sexual union before. For example, a Protestant man married a Catholic woman before a justice of the peace. This marriage is not recognized as valid by the Catholic Church. They had four children over the years. The wife is injured in a fire at home, and they call to the hospital a Catholic priest in order to convalidate their union. The marriage becomes thereby a valid, sacramental, Catholic bond. During the months of hospitalization the wife meets a Catholic hospital employee and refuses to return to her husband. Since the marriage of the mother of the four children had technically not been consummated she can petition the pope for a dispensative dissolution.

Again, members of the armed forces of the United States contract marriages by proxy when the bridegroom is stationed overseas and wishes to marry his fiancée at home. Sometimes

1. T. L. Bouscaren and A. C. Ellis, *Canon Law. A Text and Commentary,* p. 604.
2. A marriage in which one or both partners had decided to make use of contraceptive devices in order permanently to exclude children could be considered invalid because an essential element was lacking in their intention.

this is desired because she is expecting his child. Civil and ecclesiastical law permits him to appoint a proxy who will exchange vows in his stead. If their separation lasts too long, either spouse might become unfaithful and become attached to another person and later refuse to begin married life. Such a marriage was not consummated and can be dissolved by a dispensation of the Roman pontiff.

The procedure for dissolving such non-consummated marriages requires a petition submitted to the pope. The facts of the case have to be established by corporal inspection of medical experts, if the woman is still a virgin, and by deposition of witnesses. If an inspection by physicians cannot produce sufficient evidence, the sworn testimony of a number of character witnesses, called the *septima manus* (sevenfold hand)—who might not know anything in respect to the alleged inconsummation but who can vouch for the moral and religious integrity and credibility of the petitioners—is taken as sufficient evidence for the granting of the favor.

Examples of such dispensative dissolutions go back only to the centuries immediately following the reform movement of Cluny and the renaissance of canon law in the twelfth century. There was, of course, no need for the practice during the preceding centuries when most sections of the Western Church allowed complete divorce of consummated marriages. Only after the new universities had sufficiently established the theory of the indissolubility of marriage was there a need for a solution to the problems raised by this kind of marriages.

The relatively late acceptance in history of the dispensative dissolution of non-consummated marriages has been stressed in order to emphasize the exceptional nature this measure has in relationship to the indissolubility of Christian marriage. The exception is, as we have noted, entirely justified, and reason tells us that it would be a cruel God who would not offer a solution to his creatures in such circumstances. However, it being an exception from the great principle, this dispensative dissolution can be considered a true divorce and a breach in

125

the wall that ought first to permit theologians and then the ecclesiastical authorities to widen the passage to such an extent that many other suffering members of the Church can find relief.

7. LET GOD PUT ASUNDER

To continue his divine mission till the end of time, Jesus instituted the Church. The purpose of this institution was to help guide the lives of men, to provide them with means of salvation, and with direction as to how to raise their earthly existence to a supernatural level. The Church has not only a right but also a duty to concern herself with men in the world as they exist in concrete reality. As Robert McAfee Brown has trenchantly observed, "The church is not to be a haven of retreat from the world, but rather that instrumentality within the world where man's worldly situation can be most comprehensively understood, and where the dynamic for the transformation of the world can be most effectively transmitted. The church that exists for its own sake, rather than for the sake of the world, is bearing false witness. The concerns of man in the world, then, must be the concerns of the Church." [1]

In carrying out this mission, the Church possesses the authority necessary to accomplish her goals. These goals refer to the existence of man in precise and determined circumstances and not in some ideal state. One of these circumstances in which the Church has let her mission become more and more irrelevant relates to the need for rectifying erroneous judgments in selecting a mate. Considering human nature and the limitations set to human understanding of oneself and of others, total separation of married persons will in not a few instances be an indispensable legal institution, and as we have seen the Church has recognized and sanctioned it in respect to

1. "The End to False Witness: The Challenge."

126

several kinds of marriages. Correlated with total separation is the question whether a new marriage should be allowed or not. If it is a fundamental truth of Christianity that the merciful God so loved man that he sacrificed even his only Son for man's salvation, one can venture to say with so many Fathers that God also wants to place no absolutely insupportable burden on His children that would forbid remarriage, —of course, within certain limitations; this being so, it can be maintained that the Church is the sole authority to exercise this power for the marriage of Christians.

It may be true that the Church did not make use of her authority in the past, except in the case of non-consummated marriages, but this does not mean that she could not do so in the future. And when we speak of the perpetual avowal of total indissolubility by the Church in the past, we refer only to the Roman or Western Church. Historical documents demonstrate that the entire Christian East and various parts of the Western Church in certain centuries have permitted remarriage.

It could be also said that the Catholic Church made good use of the faculty granted her by her Founder, even when she denied up till now permission of remarriage to divorced Christians. However, changed times and circumstances suggest today a moderating of this attitude. This does not preclude, though it is difficult to envision such a change, the possibility that future centuries might advise the Church to return to a stricter position. As institutionalized religion becomes more and more separated from its connection with the political life of nations, and individual responsibility in this sphere is intensified, the influence of the secular world exerts its force in the shaping of minds much more than it did in times ago. It is an undeniable fact that people today are not the same as a century ago, although human nature may remain essentially unalterable.

One example we have already encountered in this evolution from strictness to leniency in the matter of divorce has occurred within the Church in our own day. Only fifty years ago, in canon 1120, n. 2, of the Code it was expressly stated that the

127

Church would not grant a dispensative dissolution of marriage between a Catholic and a non-baptized person (disparity of cult), contracted before a Catholic priest with a papal dispensation.[2] However, today such dispensative dissolutions are given by the Holy Office without any difficulty. The reason for this reversal of such a recent law is in the first place the generally now admitted principle that suffering members should be assisted as far as possible.

The tradition that the Church possesses ample authority in the province of marriage law is evidenced in the first centuries more frequently than in later epochs because the need then to develop and evolve the basic principles was greater. Today, after so many problems have been clarified by the endeavors of nearly two thousand years of theological studies, there are fewer instances in which the Church is called upon to make use of her power of the keys in order to legislate on matters of principles. Such legislation is what the Western Church actually carried out in the last five centuries in developing the so-called Petrine Privilege (Privilege of the Faith) and the dispensative dissolution of non-consummated sacramental marriages.

However, we may go much further back; for we can explain St. Paul's permission to divorce an unbelieving marriage partner under certain conditions, only by assuming that he made use of the power of the keys. He himself admits, in granting this prerogative: "To the rest I say, not the Lord ..." (1 Cor. 7, 12). Had he had a vision or a prophetic revelation? If he had felt that his concession could be derived from the teaching of Jesus, he would have indicated so. He must have regarded his permission as a novelty which could not be deduced directly from the then prevalent teaching of the Church, and which was, literally speaking, in apparent opposition to the words of Jesus, as Paul had heard them from others. Nevertheless, he

2. "This Privilege is not to be applied to a marriage between a baptized party and a non-baptized party contracted with dispensation from the impediment of disparity of worship" (canon 1120 #2; also canon 109 #2 of Oriental marriage law).

must also have considered himself empowered on behalf of the Church to develop the law, in accordance with the spirit of mercy preached by Jesus.

It appears also to be the duty of the Church to take cognizance of the differences of personality in the subjects of the law which she administers by divine ordinance, and to accommodate the law in such a manner that their spiritual good is best served. It is naïve to assume that absolute rigorism is the best means of achieving such a goal. The possibility of complete divorce is not a concession to moral laxity. Rather, divorce is a concession to the realities of human existence.

The Church is conscious of possessing ample authority, for what other could be the meaning of that power granted to her to loose and to bind? If it refers solely to sins and their forgiveness, and to the establishment of ecclesiastical punishments, it would be necessary to reply that there are no sins which are unforgiveable, and which could never be absolutely "unloosed." If a penitent is really sorry for his trespasses of the law of God and of men, the Church cannot deny him absolution. Of course, the Church can establish certain conditions for granting absolution, as various censures; but once the penitent sincerely promises to fulfill them, he receives also full pardon.

So it seems that the power of binding and loosening has in reality a limited application even if it is not extended to a much larger field. Could it not be that this power rather refers also to a legislative authority of the Church greater than it was assumed heretofore? Could it not mean that the Church has legislative power also over the bond of marriage, and that she can decide whether one kind of marriage bond can be dissolved, while another remains for the time being indissoluble, and that later for just reasons she can alter her law? [3] Indeed, this is perhaps

3. "L'Eglise, bien que non strictement inspirée, mais habitée néanmoins par le Saint-Esprit, peut dire analogiquement 'Ce n'est pas le Seigneur, c'est mois qui dis . . .' et tirer avec autorité pastorale une conclusion logique du principe—présumé reçu du Seigneur—d'une exception de base a la loi de l'indissolubilité du mariage" (O. Kéramé, "Oecumenisme et indissolubilité du mariage," in *Le Lien,* p. 21).

129

the truly essential reason for the very existence of the Church.

The present doctrine of the Catholic Church, as expressed in various official, though not infallible, documents of several popes,[4] holds that there is no human power existing which could grant a dissolution of a sacramental, consummated marriage. This was enunciated in the Code of Canon Law: "A valid *ratum* et *consummatum* marriage cannot be dissolved by any human authority and for any reason except death" (canon 1118; canon 107 of Oriental marriage law). If an authority is characterized as "human" this could refer either to its origin or to its exercise. We have already suggested that while the power to dissolve such marriages is divine in origin, God could have delegated the exercise to the Church which wields it vicariously, as is the case with non-sacramental marriages dissolved by the Church. Antoninus Abate, O.P., admits that the Church enjoys such power in relationship to natural non-sacramental marriages and sacramental, non-consummated ones, but so far as consummated, sacramental marriages are concerned papal documents seem to deny her such authority:

[The Church] does not act by virtue of her proper power, which, though divinely granted, is human in nature, since she is not acting as the principal cause, but in a merely instrumental capacity. It is certain that even a ratified and consummated marriage could be dissolved by divine power exercised directly by God, who, as legislator, can dispense from the law of indissolubility which he himself made. It is not possible, however, to assert with equal certainty that such a marriage can be dissolved by the same power, ministerially exercised by the Church, without her going beyond the limits of competency signified and intended by Christ.[5]

Following William R. O'Connor, we have already applied the distinction between intrinsic and extrinsic dissolubility of

4. For example, Pius IX and Pius XII. See A. Abate, *The Dissolution of the Matrimonial Bond in Ecclesiastical Jurisprudence*, pp. 31 f.

5. *Ibid.*, p. 31. G. G. Martinez ("Indisolubilidad del matrimonio rato y consumado," in *Revista Española de Derecho Canonico*) is also of the opinion that the "nulla humana potestate" of canon 118 includes the supreme authority in the Church.

marriage to the question whether the Church possesses the authority to grant extrinsic dissolutions of sacramental, consummated marriages. The dispensative dissolution of natural marriages in virtue of the so-called Pauline Privilege and the Privilege of the Faith granted by the Church are instances of extrinsic dissolution for which the authority must in every case come from God. In the Old Testament this power was granted through Moses also to husbands. In the New Testament there is no such explicit reference to an authority entrusted to the Church which would justify explicitly the Petrine Privilege. If the Church makes use of such authority then, it can only be because of the general, all-encompassing authority granted to her in the power of the keys (Mt. 16, 19; 18, 18).

Similarly, the great canonist Felix M. Cappello, S.J., who otherwise repeated the standard teaching of the Western Church on indissolubility, conceded the extensive authority of the Church in the province of marriage when he wrote: "Christ the Lord conferred upon Peter and his successors, in order to provide for the utility and the needs of the Church and of all the faithful, the fullness of power which is expressed by this large and unlimited formula: 'Whatever you shall bind, . . . whatever you shall loose . . .'—'Feed my lambs, feed my sheep.' " [6] And Cardinal Billot found the "binding" and "loosing" exemplified in the modes of applying ecclesiastical jurisdiction to the dissolution of sacramental, non-consummated marriages by solemn religious profession.[7] There is no reason why this power of the keys should apply to some kinds of marriages, and even to one kind of sacramental marriage, but not to all, because "the power of loosing is unrestricted—'whatever you shall loose'—and the bond of marriage that we are here considering certainly comes within its ambit." [8]

With regard to the question whether the consummated Christian marriage actually comes under the power of the keys,

6. *Op. cit.*, p. 748.
7. *De Ecclesiae Sacramentis*, p. 442.
8. O'Connor, *art. cit.*, p. 717.

131

Billot answers in the negative, but admits that the Gospels, in reporting the words of Jesus, do not warrant the distinction made by Catholic theologians in marriages which are dissoluble and others which are not. He also asserts that this has never been defined formally by any ecumenical council.[9]

O'Connor insists on the acceptance of one supreme principle: that the dissolubility of all kinds of marriages is governed by the same law. If we agree that sacramental, consummated marriages are extrinsically indissoluble because of a divine law, then this norm would apply equally to the other kinds of marriages as well; and if the Church feels that the power of the keys extends to the latter ones, it applies also to the former. The *de facto* indissolubility of consummated Christian marriage is therefore a result of the decision of the Church in the exercise of the divine power of the keys:

Does this mean that the indissolubility of a ratified, consummated marriage is only of ecclesiastical law, simply because it is the Church that binds it? Not unless we are prepared to say that the extrinsic dissolubility of those other marriages is only of ecclesiastical law simply because it is the Church that looses them. If however those other marriages are dissolved by divine law consequent upon the exercise of the power of the keys, does it not follow that a *matrimonium ratum et consummatum* is extrinsically indissoluble by divine law consequent upon the same power of the keys but exercised now in a different direction—to bind and not to loose? When and where has the Church bound this marriage? She has bound it through her constant practice of never granting a dispensation in such a marriage. . . .

The command of the Lord, as we have seen, refers primarily to the intrinsic indissolubility of marriage and as such it is a command in the strict sense. We can point to no similar command in the strict sense that would make only a ratified, consummated marriage and no other extrinsically indissoluble, but the Church has never lost sight of the ideal of primitive marriage held up by Christ as the norm for His followers at least. . . .

She effectively binds this class of marriages when by a positive

9. *Op. cit.,* p. 443.

132

act of her will she refuses to loose or dissolve them, and when she so acts she is exercising the power of the keys—a divine law given to her by Christ himself. Are we not then justified in saying that the extrinsic indissolubility of a ratified, consummated marriage is of divine law following the exercise of the power of the keys to *bind,* in the same way that the extrinsic dissolubility of all other marriages is likewise of divine law but following the exercise of the power of the keys to *loose?* If the divine law *(jus divinum)* is that which is established by God and made known to man by revelation, there can be no question but that the dissolution of a marriage through the power of the keys is of divine law. The power of the keys however works both ways—it *binds* as well as *looses.* If therefore the Church through the power of the keys binds a ratified, consummated marriage, it is bound likewise by divine and not merely ecclesiastical law.

Inasmuch as all marriages are contracts, even though some of them are sacramental and consummated, they all come under the power of the keys—provided, of course, that at least one of the parties to the contract is a subject of the Church. *In actu primo,* therefore, even ratified, consummated marriages form no exception to this unlimited power and control given by Christ to the Church. *In actu secundo,* however, these marriages are extrinsically indissoluble *de jure divino* simply because the Church has used her divinely given binding power upon them instead of her loosing power.[10]

10. *Art. cit.,* pp. 719–721. It is to be added that O'Connor saw no possibility that the Church would change her attitude: "It is the binding power of the keys that makes marriage extrinsically indissoluble. Its symbolism and the ideal of extrinsic indissolubility upheld by Christ are *motives* that induced the Church from the very beginning to use the power of the keys to bind and not to loose it. Having once committed herself to its extrinsic indissolubility there need be no fear that at some future time she may reverse herself and dissolve a marriage of this kind" (p. 721).

L. C. de Lery treats of the power of the keys, but applies it only to non-sacramental and non-consummated marriages.

R. Charland, on the contrary, in the as yet unpublished continuation of an article ("Le pouvoir de l'Eglise sur les liens du Mariage," in *Revue de Droit Canonique*) which he graciously put at my disposal, comes to the same conclusion as that which I propose, namely, that the Holy See possesses the authority to dissolve all marriages without any distinction.

One should be grateful to O'Connor for having quite cogently shown that at least the Church does possess such divine authority.

But some other considerations should be added. The existence of a visible institution, the Church, must have a much wider meaning for Christianity and humanity as such. It seems to be insufficient, even unworthy of her Founder to assume that it is only an organization to further institutional aims, as, for example, missionary activity, magisterial teaching, or administration of sacraments. For obviously such work can effectively be carried on through the centuries without being incorporated in and exercised by an all-embracing organizational Church. Islam, Judaism, and other religious movements continue to exist without such an institutional structure, without authorities empowered to decide disputed questions with finality; these movements exist simply in virtue of a common origin and common fundamental beliefs, and at the same time they all function as teaching and propagating institutions. To the Church all these faculties and tasks were given by her Founder, but with one more, namely, to legislate authoritatively and with no limit except what justice and the needs of each historical era demand. Only in this way can provision be made for all possible contingencies through the centuries. If everything has been preordained by Christ, why should an organization such as the Church be needed at all? But because the varying vicissitudes of times lead to the utility, advisability, and even necessity of changes in the rules of life for Christians, therefore a flexible, changing institution was indispensable to satisfy these needs. The Church is the *living* body of Christ, his continuation among men till the end of all time, for the needs of every time.

Once we have assumed for the Church the authority to grant total divorce, the problem presents itself of establishing limits to the exercise of this power. The Eastern Churches grant divorce on the ground of adultery of one spouse. This will usually suffice, because when a marriage case is brought before an ecclesiastical tribunal the marriage in question has been as a rule dissolved either by actual separation or by civil divorce, and at least one of the spouses has remarried according to civil law. This in itself in the Church's eyes constitutes adultery. However, there are instances when neither partner has as yet remarried or entered upon a new union. If adultery, strictly speaking, or remarriage, is then the only means of obtaining permission to remarry, the spouse desirous of contracting a new marriage might be tempted to commit adultery solely for the purpose of making the law applicable to himself. Therefore, besides the ground of adultery, supplemental reasons must be added, such as total and irrevocable separation of the spouses—made permanent perhaps by a civil divorce—if it has lasted longer than a certain period of time to be determined by law.

This was the practice of the Eastern Churches. Because in many countries the secular power recognized the judicial sentences of the Church, the non-Catholic Eastern Churches had to go beyond the ground of adultery to accept a number of other possible reasons for estrangement and separation among spouses. For this they have been criticized because it is evident that many such grounds have nothing in common with adultery as such. However, today the situation is different because in nearly all nations the state alone grants divorces, and when the spouses then approach the Church for permission to receive the religious blessing, physical adultery has already occurred either by concubinage or by remarriage, according to civil law or the law of another religious denomination.

It would not be practical to make the granting of permission to remarry contingent on the determination which partner was responsible for the breakdown of the marriage. All those who have been associated in their professional work with unsuccessful marriages, judges, attorneys, marriage counselors, and especially the clergy, know only too well that there are few unhappy marriages in which one partner is to be blamed exclusively. The usual case is that in which the lines of

135

demarcation between the culpability of one and that of the other are so indistinct that it is impossible to establish who is guiltier, while it is clear that both suffer from a number of personality deficiencies for which they often cannot be held responsible due to extrinsic circumstances. It would also not be just to take the adultery—with or without remarriage—of one spouse as presumptive proof of guilt. It could well be that the other spouse contributed largely through his or her behavior, although he himself refrains from duplicating the offense.

To propose that remarriage be permitted does not mean that divorce should be encouraged, any more than for theologians to define the various exceptions to the divine law forbidding the killing of human beings is to encourage murder; in both cases, it is simply a matter of applying the law in the contingencies of concrete cases.

Thus, when it is asked who in the Church should exercise the authority of granting a complete dissolution of the bond of Christian marriage, the answer is not necessarily that it ought to be reserved to the Holy See. It should be assumed that this power reposes with the entire Church, because it exists for the benefit of the entire Church. Of course, the actual assignment of its exercise will be governed by the supreme moderating jurisdiction of the pope. He will, in consultation with the bishops, decree who will be empowered or delegated to decide in this matter, whether an office attached to the assembly of the bishops of a nation, or regional, provincial, or metropolitan tribunals, or the courts of each diocese.

In the difficult task of establishing the limits within which the Church would grant divorces, the laity should find its proper employment, since no one else could be more competent in judging the difficulties of married life and the consequences of either denying or granting divorce. Also because of local variations in the circumstances of life, which influence so much the outcome of a marriage, it would be inadvisable not to enact legislation for the universal Church, but rather to let regional legislative bodies assisted by elected representatives of the laity

136

formulate such laws as would be appropriate for a particular area. Regulations which will have been adopted through the cooperation of dedicated laymen will be more readily obeyed and accepted than those which are imposed by the hierarchy or clergy alone. Once the hierarchy of the Church has resolved the doctrinal question as to whether or not divorce is permissible, the formulation of the exact limitations is a task in which the hierarchy has only an indirect competence, and the determination of practical details could be largely put into the hands of lay people.

APPENDIXES

I.

THE WITNESS OF THE FATHERS

St. Justin Martyr (†c. 165), who died as a martyr in Rome after a fruitful apostolate in Asia Minor, wrote two apologies in defense of Christianity in which he spoke of marriage. In the *First Apology* [1] he states: "He who marries her who has been put away by another man commits adultery." This is usually taken to mean that divorce was never and in no case permitted, though in fact it only reiterates the current conviction which forbade a wife to remarry under any condition, while it permitted a husband who had dismissed an adulterous wife to remarry.[2]

Hermas is the author of the book called the *Shepherd* (2nd c.), a work which had great authority in the early centuries and was by some ranked with holy Scripture. Hermas's aim was to preach repentance and to introduce something which he considered a novelty, namely, that the fallen Christian who had committed one of the capital sins, generally regarded as permanently ineradicable, —apostasy, murder, adultery—, could receive absolution of the sin once. Hermas avoids treating of dogma, and when he touches it he is vague and incorrect:

4. Hermas said to the messenger of God: If one has a wife who believes in the Lord, and if he apprehends her in adultery,

---

1. *PG* 6, 349.
2. In the *Second Apology* (*PG* 6, 444 f.), there is mention of a dissolution of marriage which seems, according to the opinion of many, to refer not to divorce but to simple separation. Although a second marriage was certainly excluded, we must reject the explanation that it is the case of a simple separation from bed and board since, as we have seen above, this legal institution was not known to any legislation of the time.

does he commit a sin if he lives with her? 5. And he said to me: He does not commit a sin as long as he is unaware of this misconduct, but if, knowing of the misconduct, the husband lives with his wife without her doing penance, he participates in her sin and her adultery. 6. What, then, shall the husband do, O Lord, if his wife persists in this passion? And the Lord replied: Let him put her away and let the husband abide alone; but if, after putting away his wife, he shall marry another, he likewise commits adultery . . . 8. For the sake of her repentance, therefore, the husband ought not to marry.[3]

The strictness of verse 6 seems softened somewhat by verse 8, in which the husband is counseled, not ordered, to refrain from remarrying. Rather than a legal norm, it is more an advice to people who aim at higher ideals, in conformity with the contents of the entire book.

Athenagoras, an Athenian philosopher who had become a Christian, stated around the year 177 in his *Embassy for the Christians:* "For whoever shall put away his wife and marry another, commits adultery." But concerning any second marriage he says: "Who rids himself of his first wife, although she is dead, is an adulterer in a certain disguised manner." [4]

One must be aware of the fact that Athenagoras was defending the Christians against the charges of immorality of which they were accused because of their living apart from the rest of the population and because of the "discipline of the secret." Thus he exaggerated in the direction of strictness and even called second marriage, lawfully contracted after the death of the spouse, "nothing else than decent adultery"—a preposterous notion that cancels the doctrinal value of his view on divorce.

Clement of Alexandria, who died around 217, emphasized in his *Stromata* [5] that the words of Christ in respect to marriage

3. *Opera Patrum Apostolicorum,* vol. I, p. 394.
4. *PG* 6, 965.
5. *PG* 8, 1178 and *Corpus Scriptorum Ecclesiasticorum Graecorum* 15, 219.

and continence cannot be understood by all, because they are counsels addressed to a select minority who wish to live according to "the way of the Gospel." He wrote: "What those who questioned him [Jesus] wished to know was whether a man who had discovered his wife in the act of adultery and who has therefore dismissed her, is permitted to marry another." Clement found in the Gospel only one answer: the counsel to keep continence. He referred here to the example of athletes who abstain voluntarily from any sexual intercourse. It is therefore a counsel and not a command. Clement did not say whether he condemned absolutely those who have not the courage or who do not feel called to follow this counsel of Christ, but he recommended indulgence towards them.[6]

Tertullian († 247), the great writer of the African Church, could not avoid speaking of marriage, especially when he had become an adherent of the rigorist sect of the Montanists, who among other exaggerations forbade all second marriages. But before he left the unity of the Church he affirmed in his book *Against Marcion* [7] the permissibility of divorce: *"Habet itaque et Christum assertorem iustitia divortii"* (The justification of divorce has even Christ as defender). He showed against Marcion that there is no discrepancy between Moses and Jesus on this account, but he denied that Jesus permitted divorce if a husband dismisses his wife in order to be able to marry another; the only valid reason for divorce is adultery.[8]

In his *Letter to the Wife* he spoke of widows and divorced women who had remarried. He apparently treated both ways of terminating a marriage, death and divorce, on an equal footing, disapproving of remarriage in general and not par-

6. "You shall not put away your wife except for fornication, and [Holy Scripture] considers as adultery a remarriage while the other separated person survives" (*PG* 8, 1096). While this text could refer also to the innocent husband, it is submitted that it could be better understood, in view of the contemporary social and legal customs, as referring solely to divorced wives, especially if they were guilty of adultery and therefore deprived of the right of remarriage.

7. *PL* 2, 473 f.

8. *PL* 1, 1289.

143

ticularly because of the divorce. His objection was directed against them because they rejected thereby a higher life of continence, and especially against those among them who forgot themselves so far as to marry pagans: "Now, with reference to human frailty, let us speak of another kind of conduct. We are compelled to do this because of the example of certain women who, when having been offered the opportunity of practicing continence by reason of divorce or the death of the husband, not only rejected the opportunity of such a perfect life, but in remarrying were not even mindful of the rule that they should above all marry in the Lord." [9]

Later as a Montanist he considered all second marriages, even of widowed persons, unlawful, and it cannot be expected from him that he would approve of divorce with the right of remarriage for any reason whatever: "They enter into adulterous unions even when they do not put away their wives; we are not allowed even to marry, although we put our wives away." [10] In other words, a repudiated woman cannot remarry, and second marriages are forbidden, even after the death of the spouse.

Origen of Alexandria (183–254) was one of the most learned of all Christian writers of the primitive Church, and one to whom it will be necessary to pay special attention, not only because of his encyclopedic knowledge and the fact that with him we are quite close to apostolic times, but also because of the detailed nature of his testimony. Origen reported on a tradition, lenient towards divorce, already established in his time, and gives us also his own viewpoints on the matter. The latter has been avidly commented on by theologians intent on proving the existence of a prohibition of divorce in the ancient Church.

The passage of Origen which we study here is his commentary on Matthew 19, 1–12.[11] He suggested that the original

9. *PL* 2, 991. See also 941.
10. *PG* 13, 1231 ff., and *Corpus Scriptorum* 38, 321 ff.
11. For over two centuries the majority of theologians relied on the translation of Delarue which in *PG* is set alongside the Greek text. This

marriage at the creation of Eve is a symbol of the marriage between Christ and the synagogue. Since the synagogue deserted Jesus, and even contributed to his death, he repudiated her, and took another spouse, the Church. In doing this he remained faithful to the decree of the Father, "What God has joined together, let no man put asunder," because there is one exception to this seemingly absolute prohibition of divorce, namely, the clause in Matthew 19, 9, "except for unchastity." It was the synagogue which deserted him, and thereby made the exception applicable.

From this comparison it is apparent that Origen regarded divorce and remarriage as permissible. And he concluded by noting that in holy Scripture we find certain passages which reveal not so much the transcendence of the divine as its *condescension* (*symperipheromenoi*) with regard to the frailty of the subjects of the law. This double dimension is found in the law of Moses as well as in the law of Jesus. As Moses took cognizance of the "hardness of heart" among his people and permitted them to repudiate their wives, so also did Paul when he manifested a like condescension by permitting second marriages to all except the clergy.

Origen passed then to a particular case: "Even now (*êdê*), here acting outside of holy Scripture, some superiors of the Church [that is, bishops] have permitted to a woman to [re]marry while her husband is alive; they act most assuredly outside of holy Scripture in which we read, 'The wife is bound for her lifetime to her husband,' and 'The wife will be considered adulterous if she, during the lifetime of her husband, joins up

---

translation, however, is deficient. Here, the connective particle *êdê* is given an adversative meaning (*iam vero*), while it has in fact a consecutive one (*enim*). Delarue's translation, then, would imply that Origen opposes such a solution, whereas in fact he wishes to offer it as an example of the merciful condescension permitted to the Church in the New Testament as it was to Moses in the Old. Delarue then translates *symperiphora* with *alieno arbitrio morem gerens,* while the actual meaning is "indulgence," "consideration," "condescension," in a sense used even today to describe the gracious, accommodating, and indulgent demeanor of a superior towards an inferior.

with another man.' Yet, they did not act without reason [*ou alogoos*] because, so it seems, they have accorded condescension [*symperiphora*] outside of what had been prescribed and transmitted in order to prevent worse consequences." [12]

Replying then to objections of a Jew, Origen reminded him, that "Our Lord has permitted dissolution [*dialyein*] [of the marriage bond] solely in the case of a wife convicted of misconduct," and he gave as reason: "Every husband who repudiates his wife puts her on the road to adultery, obviously excepting the case when she herself was already an adulteress." Origen concluded: "Adulterous is a woman who remarries while her husband is alive, and adulterous is the man who marries her who was repudiated."

In conclusion, it can be said that Origen was a witness to an ecclesiastical practice of indulgence in favor of a woman remarried after she was abandoned by her husband without justification. He affirmed that this practice was not without reason, although it was opposed to the text of holy Scripture. He justified it by the authority of merciful condescension possessed by the Church in the same manner as it had been exercised by Moses in the Old Testament. Origen said nothing of a husband who remarries after he has been abandoned by his wife without justification. But in view of the foregoing example, and the addition of "except for unchastity" in Matthew 19, 9, which produces a dissolution (*dialyein*) of the marriage in the case of adultery of the wife, we have no doubt that he would have been even more indulgent in this instance.

St. Cyprian, bishop of Carthage († 278), observed:

The wife shall not separate from the husband, or, if she separates, she shall remain unmarried; Paul to the Corinthians. To those, however, who have married, not I but the Lord commands that the wife shall not separate from the husband, but if she

---

12. *Testim. ad Quirinum,* III, n. 40 (Ed. Maur.), p. 326.

separates, she shall remain unmarried or shall be reconciled to the husband, and the husband shall not dismiss his wife.[13]

This passage was clearly directed against unjustified divorce, that is, one in which there is no question of adultery. It also forbids the remarriage of the wife, but does not mention the husband, a quite unexpected omission at a point where it would have been anticipated that Cyprian say something about the innocent husband's remarriage, either permitting or forbidding it. We conclude, therefore, that it cannot be deduced from this passage that St. Cyprian considered the remarriage of an innocent husband invalid.

St. Hilary, bishop of Poitiers at the beginning of the fourth century, wrote in his *Commentary on Matthew* [14] around 355:

For since the [Mosaic] law had conceded the right to divorce by the authority of a writ, now the evangelic precept proposes to the husband not only the command of peace but also makes him accountable for the very transgression of the wife who was compelled to adultery if she had to marry another man because she had been deserted, by prescribing no other ground for terminating the marriage besides that which would defile a man because of association with a prostitute wife.

While the law of Moses had permitted the husband to use a writ of divorce, the Gospel has entirely changed the requirements. It demands good will and forgiveness, and it declares guilty the husband who has deserted an innocent wife, compelling her out of necessity to remarry another man. The Gospel recognizes only two grounds for divorce and remarriage: adultery of the wife, in respect to the husband since a husband would be defiled by continuing marriage with such a wife; and desertion by the husband, in respect to the wife.

Lactantius (4th c.), a teacher of rhetoric, became a Christian when he went from Africa to Nicomedia in Minor Asia in order

13. *PL* 6, 1080.
14. *PL* 6, 720.

to become tutor of Constantine's son, Crispus, with whom he then travelled to Trier in Germany. In his *Institutionum Divinarum Libri* he says:

These are reasons why God commanded continence. However, lest somebody should believe that the divine precepts could be evaded, they are added in order that every artifice and opportunity of fraud be removed: that he is an adulterer who married a wife dismissed by her husband, and he who dismissed a wife, except for the crime of adultery, in order to take another woman. God did not want that a body be divided and cut up in pieces.[15]

In his *Epitome Divinarum Institutionum* Lactantius states:

However, as the wife is constrained by the obligation of chastity not to desire another man, so also the man is held to the same law, because God has joined man and wife in the bond of one only body. He commanded therefore not to dismiss a wife except if proven guilty of adultery, and that the bond of the conjugal contract never be dissolved except that which perfidy has broken.[16]

These two passages show that Lactantius considered adultery on the part of the wife a lawful reason for the husband to divorce her. Although he does not say so explicitly, he permitted thereby the husband to contract a new marriage, because otherwise he would have felt obliged to contradict the civil law and the custom of everyday life. According to him, the *coniugalis foederis vinculum* is dissolved or broken by the criminal behavior of the wife (*"quod perfidia ruperit"*).

St. Basil (*c*. 330–379), bishop of Caesarea and metropolitan of Cappadocia, has always enjoyed the highest regard both in the Eastern and in the Western Church. For the present purpose it is sufficient to show that this great teacher of the

15. *PL* 6, 1080.
16. Those who wish at all costs to interpret St. Basil's "embarassing" teaching on the permissibility of divorce as actually condemning it, must express themselves in the manner of Souarn: "Saint Basile s'exprime d'une façon assez difficile a comprendre bien qu'il ne contredise pas, semble-t-il, les enseignements que nous avons recueillis de la bouche des autres Pères" (*art. cit.*, col. 481).

Church expressly knew and approved of second marriages while the first spouse was still alive. If he sanctioned in some instances total divorce as understood today, and did not exclude the legal consequence of permitting a second marriage, he followed the practice of the Church of his time, as he himself confessed it, although he personally might have wished to oppose it.

In the second half of the fourth century in the Church of Cappadocia there was a penitential tradition which the saint mentioned in his letters to Amphilochius, bishop of Iconium, written in 374–375, a few years before his own death. These three letters form a whole, divided later into 85 canons,[17] of which a great number concern marriage discipline. Basil himself states that many of these regulations "have been established by our fathers, who wished to be compliant with a sweet indulgence to the frailties of those who let themselves be buried in evil" (canon 18; see canons 9, 10, 13, 34, 77, 80). They are witnesses to a pastoral tradition that is called by Basil *"the usage of the Church"* (canon. 9) or simply *"the custom"* (canons 18, 21, *et passim*). Other canons (46, 48) reflect the personal view of Basil, and in these he employed such expressions as "I do not know if . . ." (canon 9), "It appears to me . . ." (canon 28), "In my view . . ." (canon 48), and so forth.

Because of the great authority of St. Basil, it will be necessary to study his teaching on the possibility of remarriage for divorced Christians in detail. It should be stated that in his time the meaning of the legal term "adultery" was identical in Roman law and in ecclesiastical law, and refers *solely* to the illegitimate union of a man, married or not, to a married woman. The relationship of a married or unmarried man to an unmarried woman is fornication.

The extramarital transgressions of a husband are not adulterous:

17. See *PG* 32, 675 ff.

Canon 21. If a married man does not content himself with his marriage and falls into misconduct we condemn his as fornicator and we impose upon him the largest punishments. However, we have no canon that could permit to raise against him the accusation of adultery if the sin was committed with a woman herself free of marriage.

The wife is not entitled to leave an adulterous husband:

Canon 9. Sacred Scripture says however of the adulteress: 'She who is tainted lives as defiled and shall not return to her husband' (Jer 3,1) and also: 'He who retains an adulteress is foolish and irreligious' (Prov 18,22), but, on the other hand, it does not forbid the husband guilty of fornication to live with his wife. On the contrary, the wife is obliged to receive back her husband who returns from his fornication, while the husband will chase away her who has defiled herself. It is not easy to find a reason for this practice, but such is the custom which has prevailed.

Illegal remarriage can be condoned after penance:

Canon 77. He who has deserted a woman with whom he was lawfully united in order to take another is certainly subject to condemnation as an adulterer in virtue of the sentence of the Lord; but it was decided by our Fathers that the culpables ones shall do penance as weepers [*flentes*] for one year, that they shall be hearers [*audientes*] two years, and *prostrati* three years; that the seventh year they shall stand with the faithful, and they shall be judged worthy of the offering if they have done penance with tears.

The innocent wife abandoned by her husband cannot remarry:

Canon 48. The wife who was abandoned by her husband ought in my view remain alone. Indeed, the Lord said: 'Whoever abandons his wife, except for fornication, makes her commit adultery.' Now, it is a fact that he [Christ] called her an adulteress, and forbade her a union with another man. How, indeed, can the man appear to be accused to encourage the adultery of the woman if she can be exempt from reproach, she who was called adulterous by the Lord on account of her union with another man?

In maintaining that this woman should "remain alone"

150

Basil gave his personal opinion, which he justified further from the text of Matthew 5, 32. However, from the way he offered his opinion it seems that this practice was not followed by the Church but that Basil endeavored to introduce it (see also canon 46).

The unjustly abandoned husband can be forgiven if he re-marries:

Canon 35. In the case of a husband who has been abandoned it will be necessary to examine the cause for the desertion. If it is manifest that the woman left without justification, the husband is worthy of forgiveness, and the woman deserves punishment. Forgiveness will be accorded to such a husband, provided he is in communion with the Church.

The husband who is spoken of here is one who has remarried; otherwise, there would be nothing for which he would have to be forgiven. This can be deduced also from canon 9 where Basil says that "a woman who lives with another man," himself abandoned, "is not condemned." Therefore, it follows that "the man is justified too" (canon 9) and "worthy of forgiveness" (canon 48) if he takes another wife, while his wife who has deserted him is culpable and therefore "worthy of punishment" (canon 9).

The legal inequality of sexes accepted by custom:

Canon 9. The declaration of the Lord, that it is not permitted to separate a marriage except for the cause of fornication [*parektos logou porneias*] applies equally to men as to women, if one considers the logical consequence of the idea. However, the custom is different, and we find many more demands imposed upon women.

On the remarriage of the unjustly abandoned husband:

Canon 9 (cont.). The Apostle said: "He who united himself with a prostitute becomes one sole body with her." Jeremiah: "If a woman joins another man she shall not return to her husband, but being defiled she shall remain defiled." And also: "He who keeps an adulteress is a fool and an irreligious man." But the custom also orders adulterous men and those who are in the state

151

of fornicators not to forsake their wives. *This is why, if one of these was abandoned [by his spouse], I do not say that one can treat as an adulteress the woman who afterwards marries him.* Indeed, the culpable one is here the wife who has deserted her husband. For what reason has she left him? Was she beaten and could not suffer the blows? It would have been better to endure then to separate from her spouse. Would she have suffered damage to her fortune which she could not tolerate? The excuse is still insufficient. It is because that man has given himself to fornication? Still, we have no such observance [*paraterema*] in the customary law of the Church. Even the infidelity of a pagan husband is not a sufficient ground for his wife to leave him. She has, on the contrary, the duty to remain with him, on account of the incertitude of the result; since "do you know, woman, that you will save your husband?" This is why the wife who has left her husband is an adulteress if she joins another man. As to the husband who was abandoned, it can be excused [if he remarries], and the woman who lives with him under such conditions is not condemned. Nevertheless, if the man himself has abandoned his [innocent] wife, and if he has joined up with another, then he himself is an adulterer, because he has made his legitimate wife commit adultery; and she who cohabits with him is also adulterous because she attracted the husband of another woman.

This manner of pastoral thinking, so Christian and so humane at the same time, might seem somewhat strange to the Western spirit, which is often inclined to favor legalistic solutions. To illustrate this practice of "tolerance" on the part of St. Basil, two other canons may be cited, one on fornication and the other on the problem of third marriages.

Fornication or the informal beginning of a marriage is forgiveable:

Canon 26. Fornication is not marriage; it is not even the beginning of marriage. That is why, if it is possible to induce to separate those who have united themselves in fornication, this is the best thing to do. But if they absolutely desire to live together, the penance reserved for fornication shall be imposed upon them, yet without separating them, lest something worse should result.

152

We must assume that such a couple was prevented from legalizing their marital union because of a former marriage by either partner. But if they cannot be persuaded to dissolve their informal union, it can be validated provided they submit to ecclesiastical penance.

A third marriage can be accepted by the Church:

Canon 50. There is no law [permitting] the third marriage. This is why the third marriage is not contracted according to the law. Some of us regard such practice as defilement of the Church, but we do not throw upon them public condemnation because we judge them preferable to unbridled fornication.

St. Basil must have understood under "fornication" and "trigamy" marital unions which were not marriages in the eyes of the Church, because otherwise he could not have considered them invalid. They may defile the Church, and the shepherds of the Church must deplore them, but it is not necessary publicly to condemn them. The individuals involved will be subject to penance, which means that they will ultimately receive absolution and admission to the sacraments. This implied that these unions became validated and thereby true marriages. The Eastern Fathers were not guided by a preoccupation with what juridical category the marital cohabitation of such persons could be assigned, and did not make a distinction between valid but nevertheless unlawful acts.

This manner of the Eastern Fathers of applying to practical cases the principles derived from their personal understanding of the divine law was the basis for the doctrine of *oikonomia*. This theory reserves to the Church the right in individual cases to apply the canons freely with pastoral discretion (*kat'oikonomian*) instead of deciding them in strict accord with written laws (*kat'akribeian*).

St. Gregory of Nazianzus (325–389) inveighs against the double standard of civil law in respect to the adultery of husband and wife; while the first remains unpunished, the latter is treated severely. He speaks also of the right of the husband to

153

dismiss an adulterous wife, but says nothing concerning his possibly remarrying.[18] However, he uses the Greek term *"apostasion,"* which he took from civil law, and which means total divorce and permission of remarriage.[19]

His general attitude was still against repeated marriages, even by widowed persons: "The first is the law, the second is tolerance and indulgence, the third iniquity. But he who exceeds this number is plainly a swine . . ." [20]

In his *Commentary to Matthew 19, 9,* he is concerned only with vindicating equality for the wife. This would permit the conclusion that he accepted divorce initiated by the husband but wished the same right to extend to the wife.

St. Ambrose (340–397), bishop of Milan, spoke of the wife being dismissed by the husband, but advised against it. He made no distinction between the sexes as to rights in marriage. He affirmed simply that it is not permitted "to take another wife while the first wife is alive" [*ducere uxorem, uxore vivente*], without mentioning adultery or any other divorce ground.[21]

Ambrosiaster is the name given to an anonymous author of a commentary, written around 380, on the epistles of St. Paul, which was for a long time ascribed to St. Ambrose of Milan. The author of this commentary denied to a wife any right to divorce her husband. She can separate from him because of his adultery, apostasy, or unnatural sexual demands, but if she cannot keep continence she must be reconciled with her husband. But for the husband another law exists: "A man is permitted to remarry if he has dismissed the sinning wife, because he is not limited in his rights as the woman is; after all, the head of the woman is the man." [22]

18. *PL* 39, 1151.
19. Zhishman, *op. cit.,* p. 112.
20. *PG* 36, 289 and 293; 37, 247.
21. *PL* 15, 1766–1768.
22. "Viro licet ducere uxorem, si dimiserit uxorem peccantem; quia

St. Asterius, bishop of Amasea in Pontus (Minor Asia), a great orator, wrote around 400 with great earnestness of moral conviction. In his opinion adultery and death are equivalent in their legal effect, both dissolve marriage, and consequently permit remarriage: "This you should hold as established and be entirely persuaded of, that marriage can be dissolved for no cause whatever, except because of death and adultery." [23]

St. Epiphanius, archbishop of Salamis and head of the Church on the island of Cyprus, who died in 403, wrote a book valuable for the information it contains concerning the religious history of the fourth century. His major work is the *Panarion* (Medicine Chest) a remedy against the poison of heresies, of which he counted eighty. In discussing the 59th heresy he speaks first of the second marriages of widows, which he tolerates as the lesser evil, and in conjunction with which he treats also the situation of the unfortunate spouse who was forced to separate legally from the other spouse. He says:

He who cannot keep continence after the death of his first wife, or who has separated from his wife for a valid motive, as fornication, adultery, or another misdeed, if he takes another wife, or if the wife takes another husband, the divine word does not condemn him nor exclude him from the Church or the life; but she tolerates it rather on account of his weakness. Not that this man can keep with him two wives, the first one still gravitating [*periouses*] around him; but if he is actually separated [*aposchetheis*] from his first wife, he may take another according to the law, if this is his desire.[24]

St. Chromatius († 407), bishop of Aquileia, one of the more respected bishops of his time, was in correspondence with all of his more illustrious contemporaries, such as St. Jerome,

---

non ita constringitur, sicut mulier; caput enim mulieris vir est" (*PL* 17, 218).

23. *PG* 40, 225.
24. *PG* 41, 1024 f., and *Corpus Scriptorum* 31, 368 f.

St. Ambrose, and Rufinus. There are preserved seventeen treatises by him on the Gospel according to Matthew and a homily on the eight beatitudes. Concerning the passage "What God has joined together, let no man put asunder" Chromatius said:

He [Jesus Christ] condemned, by pronouncing sentence, not only the passive permission of the Jews, but also the silly and miserable presumption of the Manichees, who deny that marriages are from God, saying: Except on account of adultery, it is not permitted to dismiss a wife; thereby clearly establishing that he acts against the will of God who recklessly presumes to separate by an illicit divorce a marriage joined together by God. . . . Therefore, they shall be aware what a grave crime, punished by God with damnation, those incur who because of their unbridled lust [without the reason of adultery] dismiss their wives and wish to pass on to other marriages. . . . They believe that they are able to do this without punishment for the reason that it seems to be permitted by human and worldly laws, ignoring the fact that they commit a more serious crime because they give preference to human before divine laws; for they believe to be legitimate that which God established to be unlawful, simply because it is freely permitted by man.

However, as it is not lawful to dismiss a wife leading a chaste and pure life, so it is also permitted to dismiss an adulterous woman, because she has rendered herself unworthy of her husband's companionship, she who by sinning with her body has dared to violate the temple of God.[25]

The only ground for dismissing a wife is adultery on her part, and the secular laws and customs which permit a husband to divorce his wife for other reasons are invalid. Husbands who remarry, although the dismissed was not guilty of adultery, are condemned. In other words, they would not be blameworthy for a second marriage if the first wife were guilty of adultery.

St. John Chrysostom (347–407), bishop of Constantinople, a doctor of the Church, spoke in several of his writings on the

25. *PL* 20, 35.

156

problem of divorce.[26] He was very much interested in elevating the moral concepts of Christians on the question of conjugal fidelity, and he considered the extramarital affairs of the husband, even with unmarried women, to be adultery.

He speaks of the prohibition against wives, even if innocently repudiated by their husbands, to enter upon a new marriage during the lifetime of the husband; but he says nothing on the much more frequent problem of husbands remarrying, especially after they had divorced adulterous wives. We cannot regard this as simple oversight, but as a witness to the existing legal system of the Church, attested by so many witnesses, which permitted a husband to remarry if he had divorced his wife because of adultery, but denied the same right to a wife.[27]

In his treatise on the writ of divorce, quoted usually as *De Libello Repudii,* [28] Chrysostom declares first that he would explain the law and then try to interpret that which is against the law. He speaks then on these prohibitions of the law: (1) The wife cannot join another man while her husband is alive. (2) The wife who was repudiated by her husband can never be married by another man. (3) A widow ought not but can, if she so wishes, remarry. (4) The wife cannot give a writ of divorce to her husband although civil law may permit it.

Since Chrysostom asserts that he will specify the law on this matter, the omission of any mention of whether the husband could or could not remarrry after he had dismissed his wife, has no explanation except that such remarriage was allowed by the Church of his time. It could be quite well that he himself did not favor this practice, but he did not speak against it in a place where one would necessarily have expected it.

26. *Homilia* 17, 4; *Homilia* 62, Mt., n. 1, 2; *Homilia* 26, Gen.; *Homilia* 17, Mt.
27. " . . . bien qu'il insiste sur l'indissolubilité absolue du lien conjugal, on ne voit pas qu'il interdise clairement à l'époux légitimement divorcé de se remarier" (J. Tixeront, *Histoire de dogmes,* vol. II, p. 192).
28. *PG* 51, 221; 57, 260.

In the succeeding pages he makes such additional statements as that "The adulterous woman is nobody's wife," [29] in other words, that adultery can dissolve the marriage bond; or "Also he who dismissed without the cause of adultery and he who took the dismissed wife while the husband was alive will be punished together with the dismissed woman." [30] Again Chrysostom misses a compelling opportunity to condemn the husband who remarried after dismissing his adulterous wife, but he does not do so.

St. Jerome (340–420) is often quoted as one who prohibits any remarriage after divorce; but this claim will appear exaggerated as the study of several passages will show.

In his letter to Amandus he says: "As long as the husband is alive, whether he is adulterous, whether he is a sodomist, whether he is covered with sins and abandoned by his wife because of all these crimes, he is considered to be the husband of her to whom it is not allowed to take another man." [31] The only conclusion one is permitted to draw from this passage is: the wife has no right ever to divorce her husband. Whether an innocent husband can abandon an adulterous wife and marry another is here neither affirmed nor denied.

In a letter to Oceanus Jerome writes about Fabiola, a Christian woman of Rome, who divorced her husband because of adultery, and then remarried. She did public penance when it was pointed out to her, after the death of the second husband, that she was not entitled to dismiss her husband:

The Lord commanded that the wife shall not be dismissed except because of fornication; and if she was dismissed, she shall remain unmarried. Whatever is commanded to men as a consequence affects women. Not even an adulterous wife should be dismissed, even if the husband is to be considered adulterous. If one joins himself to a prostitute he becomes one body with her;

29. *PG* 51, 221.
30. *PG* 51, 222.
31. *PL* 22, 560.

therefore, also that which is joined to a fornicator and impure man becomes one body with him. Different are the laws of the Caesars and those of Christ; one thing is commanded by Papinianus and something else by our Paulus. In their world the bridles of shamelessness are relaxed, and while only rape and adultery is condemned, lust is permitted far and wide in brothels and with maidservants, as if honor is blameworthy and not propensity. With us what is not permitted to women is equally not permitted to men; and the position of a slave is regarded to be of an equal condition. . . . Therefore also Fabiola, because she persuaded herself and assumed that she had lawfully dismissed her husband, did not know the legal force of the Gospel, in which every right to remarriage is taken away from women during the lifetime of their husbands. While she avoided the devil's many injuries, she received one wound because of her incautiousness. . . . Who would believe that after the death of the second husband she would turn in on herself . . . would dress in sackcloth, in order to confess publicly her error.[32]

St. Jerome emphasizes here the moral equality and equal responsibility of the sexes, and points out that the morality of secular legislators, as the Caesars, and of interpreters of civil law, as Papinianus, do not decide the question of sinfulness. However, he maintains the legal inequality, because woman is affected by the law of God through man, but not vice versa. While the husband can dismiss an adulterous wife, a wife cannot dismiss her husband even if he is an adulterer.

With the distinction between moral and legal equality or inequality, and the principle of legal inequality of the sexes in mind, there will not be found anything in this passage that would deny the husband the right of remarriage as recognized by civil and ecclesiastical law of the time. Had St. Jerome been convinced that it was improper, he would have felt obliged to refer to it in this place.

In his commentary on Matthew 19, St. Jerome says:

. . . Replying, he said: "Have you not read that he who made them from the beginning made them male and female?" This is

32. *PL* 22, 691 f.

written in the beginning of Genesis. When he said "male and female" he stated that second marriages are to be avoided. For he did not say "male and females," —what would have to be expected because of the writ of divorce existing before, but "male and female," that they should be joined in the community of one wife.[33]

In view of the idea that widowhood is the more preferable solution after the death of a spouse, further marriages were considered less proper, and it is about this that St. Jerome speaks. It cannot be applied as referring exclusively to second marriages during the lifetime of the other spouse, justifiably dismissed because of adultery, although they were included in St. Jerome's disapproval. Even less can it be deduced that a second marriage of any kind is invalid.

In the same commentary St. Jerome says:

Only fornication takes away the legal condition of a wife; since she split the one flesh asunder and separated herself from the husband by fornication, she must not be held on to, lest she should bring a curse upon the husband, as Scriptures says: "He who keeps an adulterous woman is a fool and has no religion." Whenever, therefore, there is the case of fornication or suspicion of fornication, the wife is freely dismissed. Because it could happen that a husband falsely accuses an innocent wife or that he uses criminal force with the old wife, therefore the husband is ordered to dismiss the wife on condition that he shall not have a second wife during the lifetime of the first. . . . What he said is this: If you do not dismiss the wife because of desire but on account of the injury, why then do you, who have experienced unhappiness in your first marriage, expose yourself to the peril of a new one? And because it could happen that in accordance with the same law the wife, too, could give the husband a writ of divorce, the same caution is prescribed, that she shall not take another man.[34]

Here St. Jerome expresses the conviction that a husband is not allowed to continue living with an adulterous wife. This is

33. *PL* 22, 134.
34. *PL* 22, 135.

160

based on some passages of the Old Testament, and was the opinion of a number of Fathers. These words have also been explained by some authors as containing a permission to the husband to remarry if the adultery was proved in the external forum, and a prohibition of remarriage only if there was a mere suspicion or if the husband had used force to make the wife falsely confess adultery.

Amandus had questioned Jerome concerning a wife who had left a bad husband and had married another man. To this he received this answer: "The Apostle, cutting off therefore all reasons, defined in the clearest manner that that wife is adulterous who marries another man while the husband is alive." [35] This is again a confirmation held by the ancient Church that only a husband had the right of dismissing a wife but not vice versa.

His persuasion that a husband could not receive back his wife whom he had dismissed because of adultery, St. Jerome tersely expressed thus: "If she left the second husband and wishes to be reconciled with the first, she cannot do that." [36]

St. Cyril of Alexandria († 431) declares categorically that adultery completely dissolves the marriage bond.[37] Whether remarriage was considered permitted cannot be answered from the passage, but Cyril states explicitly that "God, as I firmly believe, adapted his laws to the measure of human nature." [38]

Another passage seems to favor indissolubility: "By dismissing the wife he gives her an opportunity to remarry, which is a kind of adultery, similar to a [marriage] bond that is not yet dissolved." [39]

This is again one of those numerous witnesses from Christian

35. *PL* 22, 562.
36. *PL* 22, 563.
37. See J. B. M. Mayaud, *L'indissolubilité du mariage. Etude historico-canonique*, p. 72.
38. *PG* 74, 874.
39. *PG* 77, 379.

antiquity censuring the remarriage of the more rarely occurring adulterous wife and not mentioning at all the much more frequent male adulterer.

St. Augustine († 604) virtually established the concept of absolute indissolubility as a norm for the Western Church although centuries were to pass until his interpretation found general acceptance. Augustine was aware that the idea as formulated by him was new. In his *De conjugiis adulterinis,* written in response to an inquiry concerning wives who had separated from their husbands because of their adultery, Augustine permits separation but forbids the remarriage of either the husband or the wife due to any alleged inequality between them: ". . . nor is it permitted to the wife dismissed by the husband to marry another as long as her husband is alive, nor to a husband dismissed by the wife to take another woman, except if she who had left him has died." [40]

Augustine admits that the Gospels are not clear and he suggests that Jesus mentioned the case of infidelity only incidentally as justifying divorce, and left it to the Church to develop the legal consequences, particularly those relating to the remarriage of the husband of an adulterous wife. According to Augustine, there evolved in the Church the teaching that no remarriage is ever permitted.[41]

It is hardly necessary to recall that Augustine was involved in controversy with the Manichaeans as well as with the refutation of certain teachings of Tertullian concerning marriage, and that he may have adopted a rigid position in order not to make the Church appear as demanding a lesser degree of perfection than did the heretics. It is a commonplace that his

40. " . . . nec dimissa a viro nubere liceat alteri, quamdiu vir ejus vivit; nec dimisso ab uxore liceat alteram ducere, nisi mortua fuerit quae recessit" (*PL* 40, 455). It is strange that Augustine speaks only of the adulterous wife and the adulterous husband and overlooks the situation of the innocent husband who has dismissed an adulterous wife.

41. *PL* 40, 458. See Schleck, *op. cit.,* p. 157.

own attitude towards sexuality was both negative and mistrusting.[42] Another circumstance which diminishes the import of his witness is his failure to base it on the practice of other parts of the Church or on the opinions of other writers. Since he was by correspondence connected with many of the most distinguished churchmen of his epoch, it was not ignorance, but rather personal and therefore also arbitrary conviction which led him to introduce a line of thought that later widened the rift between the Eastern Church and the West.

His argumentation on the permissibility of divorce-remarriage is an exercise in exegesis that could hardly be accepted by any modern biblical scholar. In spite of this fact, the principles which he developed, and even his terminology, are the foundation of Western theology on marriage. Although he might not specifically say so the choice of the topics of his writings indicates the custom and the practice of the Church at his time.[43]

A proof that Augustine, too, felt the need of the Church sometimes to permit divorce is the distinction he makes when he speaks of the qualifications of candidates for baptism. He distinguishes between a man who has remarried after he divorced a wife that was apprehended in adultery, and a man who has contracted a second marriage although the wife he divorced was not guilty of adultery. Concerning the former category he says:

Also, he who dismissed a wife apprehended in adultery and married another wife seems not to deserve to be put on an even footing with those who dismiss and remarry without having as reason adultery. This is so obscure even in the divine revelation itself, whether he who is without doubt allowed to dismiss an adulterous wife is to be held to be an adulterer should he marry

42. See Noonan, *Contraception,* pp. 119–139 and Schleck, *op. cit.* pp. 44 f.
43. In this, St. Augustine differs from St. Basil, who repeatedly refers to the custom (*synetheia*) and usage of the Church, even when they are contrary to his own opinion.

another woman, that, in my judgment, anyone who strays commits in this regard only a venial fault.[44]

Writing on the sacramentality of marriage, Augustine denies that adultery itself could dissolve the marriage bond, because then the wife could simply sin to receive the benefit of divorce.[45] It must be assumed that Augustine refers to an automatic dissolution. In another place he states: ". . . it is permitted to dismiss a wife solely on account of adultery; but during her lifetime it is not allowed to take another wife." [46]

In Chapter IX of *De conjugiis adulterinis* he disinguishes all categories of divorced marriage partners: (1) The wife dismissed by her husband although no adultery on her part is charged. (2) The man who marries a woman dismissed by her husband even though adultery had not taken place. (3) The husband who dismisses his wife, who had not been charged with adultery, and then remarries. (4) The husband who dismisses an adulterous wife. The second marriage for all these categories is forbidden. However, Augustine distinguishes between the husband who remarried after he dismissed an innocent wife and one who repudiated an adulterous wife: ". . . neither, therefore, do we defend from the stain of this sin him who because of adultery dismissed and took another [wife]. Both we consider to be adulterers, although the one more seriously than the other . . ." [47]

In speaking of the problem of the legal inequality of the sexes, St. Augustine is an oblique witness to the practice of his

44. "Quisquis etiam uxorem in adulterio deprehensam dimiserit, et aliam duxerit, non videtur aequandus eis qui, excepta causa adulterii, dimittunt et ducunt; et in ipsis divinis sententiis ita obscurum est, utrum et iste, cui quidem sine dubio adulteram licet dimittere, adulter tamen habeatur si alteram duxerit, ut, quantum existimo, venialiter quisque fallatur" (*PL* 40, 221).

45. *PL* 40, 473.

46. "Solius fornicationis causa licet uxorem adulteram dimittere; sed illa vivente non licet alteram ducere" (*PL* 39, 1710).

47. " . . . nec ideo tamen eum qui propter causam fornicationis dimiserit et alteram duxerit, ab huius peccati labe defendimus. Ambos enim, licet altero gravius, moechos tamen esse cognovimus . . . " (*PL* 40, 484).

time: (1) in permitting aggrieved husbands a new marriage after divorce; (2) in denying the same right to the wives: "However, how can it be that the husband is permitted to marry another woman after he had repudiated an adulterous wife, while the wife is not [permitted] to marry another man after she has left an adulterous husband, I cannot see . . ." [48]

Another passage seems clearly to support the present Catholic teaching: ". . . . Although she has been dismissed because of fornication, she has not ceased to be the wife of the dismissing husband . . ." [49] But we find also another solution of a marriage problem by Augustine as quoted in Gratian's Decree. Speaking of a husband who could not remarry, according to the law of the Christians, as long as his [adulterous?] wife is alive, and thereby might be provoked to kill her in order to become free, Augustine is reported as suggesting that he should be permitted a new marriage: "If he is resolved on doing what is not licit, he shall sooner commit adultery than commit homicide." [50]

The conclusion to all this can only be that St. Augustine's intention was to forbid any remarriage of any divorced Christians, that he knew of the practice of the Church which allowed husbands who had dismissed adulterous wives to remarry, and that he was not above employing in extreme instances that "condescension" which the Eastern Father considered a right of the Church as the dispensor of divine mercy among men.

Theodoret (393–457), bishop of Cyrus in Syria, speaks in several places in his writings of the dissolution of marriages. He compares the ancient times, when a wife could be dismissed by her husband for no other reason than a feeling of

48. *PL* 35, 1459.
49. "Quomodo autem viro possit esse licentia ducendae alterius, si adulteram reliquerit, cum mulieri non sit nubendi alteri, si adulteram reliquerit, non video . . . " (*PL* 40, 458).
50. " . . . etiam propter fornicationis causam dimissam est, nondum emittentis uxor esse cessavit . . . " (*PL* 40, 459).

aversion on his part, with the new times, when the only reason for divorce is the wife's adultery.[51] In another passage Theodoret states that the old law was abolished and that now only fornication on the part of the wife gives the right to divorce.[52] Regarding second marriages (*peri deuterou gamou*), he mentions solely widows,[53] and so implies that the counsel of St. Paul concerning second marriages does not apply to widowers.

Victor of Antioch, who wrote in the fifth century, was inclined to recognize the validity of a new marriage entered by the husband after he had divorced his wife because of adultery.[54]

St. Avitus, bishop of Vienne (France; from about 490 to 518), mentions in a letter to a certain Anselmundus the persuasion current at his time in Gaul that a man can separate from his adulterous wife and marry another in virtue of Christ's permission.[55]

St. Theodore of Tarsus († 690), archbishop of Canterbury, a Greek by birth, was a theologian and canonist of great repute. His only extant writings are the decisions in disciplinary matters known as *Penitential of Theodore.* In it he defends his judgment that: (1) adultery on the part of the wife gives the husband the right to divorce her and to marry again, provided the divorced wife was his first one; (2) also the divorced wife can remarry after a penance of two years; and (3) a wife cannot divorce a husband not even if he committed adultery.[56] Theo-

---

51. "Si enim facturus est quod non licet, iam faciat adulterium, et non faciat homicidium" (*Corpus Iuris Canonici,* si quod, 9, caus. XXXII, q. 11).
52. *PG* 82, 276. See also *PG* 83, 505.
53. *PG* 83, 537.
54. *PG* 83, 541.
55. See Mayaud, *op. cit.,* p. 73.
56. *PL* 59, 267.

dore also states that a spouse who permits the other to enter the religious life can marry again. According to the rules observed in the Greek Church, the spouse remaining in the world qualifies for remarriage during the lifetime of the partner who had entered religious life only in the case that the marriage dissolved by the entrance into religion was the first one for him. If it was a second or successive marriage, he had to wait till the spouse in religion had died.

Another ground for divorce and remarriage mentioned in the *Penitential* arises when the husband has become a slave as a punishment for fornication or stealing (*seipsum in furto aut fornicatione servum facit*), or any other sin; the wife can marry another man after a year has elapsed if the dissolved marriage was her first.[57] In another place,[58] Theodore states that when a husband is deserted by his wife he can with the consent of the bishop remarry after five years have elapsed. If a wife was taken away into slavery, the husband can remarry after one year, but if the husband is in captivity, the wife must wait five years before she can marry again.[59] However, if the original wife or husband should return, the first marriage must be reestablished. This is not the same procedure as when the spouse disappears and is of unknown whereabouts and presumed to be dead. Theodore assumes that the wife or husband abducted into captivity is still alive, but nevertheless permits a new marriage for humanitarian reasons.

St. Bede the Venerable, (*c.* 673–735) the great historian

57. "Maritus, si se ipsum in furto aut fornicatione servum facit vel quocumque peccato, mulier, si prius non habuit coniugium, habet potestatem post annum alterum accipere virum, digamo autem non licet."

58. These excerpts and the following are found in *PL* 99, 933 ff. "Si mulier discesserit a viro suo dispiciens eum nolens revertere et reconciliari viro, post V annos cum consensu episcopi aliam accipere licebit uxorem." "Si cuius uxorem hostis abstulerit et ipse eam iterum adipisci non potest, licet aliam tollere: melius est quam fornicari."

59. "Si ab aliquo sua discesserit, I annum poeniteat ipsa, si impolluta revertatur ad eum, ceterum III annos, ipse unum si aliam duxerit."

and doctor of the Church, is probably the author of a commentary on the Gospel of St. Matthew. He says there that only God can separate what he has joined together. A man violates this when he dismisses his first wife on account of his desire for the second wife. As to the grounds for lawful separation permitted by God, there are two: a fleshly reason, namely, fornication perpetrated by the wife; and a spiritual one, the desire to enter religion. Therefore, it seems justifiable on our part to conclude from his words that if marriages are dissolved because of adultery or entrance into religion, it is God who "separates" the marriage. Because of the reference to the Old Testament, it can be deduced that the divorce mentioned by Bede has the same effect as the New Testament, namely, total dissolution of the bond and the right of remarriage for the husband.[60]

In a passage from his commentary on 1 Corinthians 7, St. Bede apparently contradicts himself and excludes the remarriage even of a husband who dismissed his wife because of adultery:

I believe for the same reason that if he dismissed one he shall not take another wife but shall be reconciled with his wife. It can happen that he dismisses his wife because of fornication, which the Lord wishes to be the exception. However, since it is not permitted to her to marry while her husband whom she left is alive, so also not to him to take another wife while the wife whom he dismissed is alive; and it is even less lawful for him to commit debauchery with anyone.[61]

St. Boniface († 755) archbishop of Mainz, decrees in his canon 35 that the priest shall caution the faithful against unlawful marriages, because the only reasons for separation are fornication and the service of God. Consequently, if these two reasons for separation are verified, marriages entered by spouses whose first marriages were dissolved either on account

60. *PL* 92, 85 f.
61. *S. Bedi Venerabilis Opera,* col. 418.

of fornication or by entrance into religion would seem to have been considered lawful.[62]

Egbert, († 766), archbishop of York, is the presumed author of canons circulated under his name. In one of them there is mentioned an African canon of unknown origin which he cites:

A lawful marriage, therefore, cannot be separated without the consent of both; however, one [spouse] can permit the other to enter the service of God with the agreement of the bishop. Some others say also: If the husband or the wife enter religious life with this consent, the other [spouse] is allowed to contract a new marriage, but only with a not-yet married girl or boy, if he [she] cannot be continent. Of this I do not approve. But if a married man wants to join a monastery, he is not to be received, except if he received permission from the wife who herself promised chastity. Hence, if she, because of incontinence, should marry another man, while the former is still alive, she commits adultery, and he who dismissed her will share in her sin.[63]

The canon quoted by Egbert permitted a second marriage only to the husband who had dismissed an adulterous wife if this had been his first marriage, a legal principle encountered also among other ancient Fathers. Egbert rejects even this permission. However, he seems to deny the right of remarriage to the spouse who remained in the world only if it is the instance of a wife whose husband entered religious life. Such an inequality, to permit the husband what is forbidden to the wife in the same condition, as we have seen, is consonant with the older canonical order of the Church.

The same idea is behind another decision: "With the consent of the bishop, he can take another wife if he cannot live continent, and he shall do penance for three years, or even as

---

62. "Admoneat unusquisque presbyterorum publice plebum . . . legitimum coniugium nequaquam posse ulla occasione separari, excepta causa fornicationis, nisi cum consensu amborum et hoc propter servitium Dei" (*PL* 89, 823).
63. *PL* 89, 392.

long as he lives because he is judged adulterous according to the opinion of the Lord." [64] This canon concerns a husband who had to emigrate because by feudal law he was obliged to follow as a vassal his liege lord. If his wife refused to follow her husband, he could marry another.

Again, there is the startling idea that the husband can validly and lawfully remarry, even though he must do penance to compensate for this special concession to his human weakness. Egbert regarded the remarriage lawful as somewhat against the wish of Christ, and therefore calls adulterous the beneficiary of this mercy.

St. Megingoz, or *Megingaud,* bishop of Würzburg in Germany between 753 and 785, worked strenuously for the Christianization of Saxony. Writing to St. Lullus, the successor of St. Boniface as bishop of Mainz, he decries the diversity of opinion among the Fathers concerning the question of divorce and remarriage. He mentions Isidore, Jerome, Augustine, and Pope Leo I. It is immaterial that the opinions attributed to Isidore and Jerome are contained in writings of other authors; they are still witnessing to the persuasion of his times on this matter. He mentions also that Leo I permitted a wife whose husband had been captured by the enemy without hope of returning to remarry on condition that she go back to him if he should return.[65] It should be pointed out that this is not a case of the presumed death of the husband since the pope had to assume that the first husband was still alive at the time of the second marriage of his wife.

Nicephorus, patriarch of Constantinople (806–815), is the author of a number of legal opinions which were edited as canons and have been accepted into the official canonical collections of the Byzantine Church. In his canons 115 and 123 he declares arbitrary divorces not to be invalid, although they

64. *PL* 99, 1156.
65. *PL* 96, 825.

170

are clearly unlawful, but subjects the guilty persons and their new marriage partners to an ecclesiastical penance lasting from three to five years.[66] Being a witness from the Eastern Church, he did not oppose divorce.

Burchard († 1025), bishop of Worms, a celebrated canonist, collected many laws between 1023 and 1025, of which we shall select two for special mention:

First, in respect to a husband who had forced his wife to commit adultery:

However, if your wife should be able to prove this, that she was used for adultery due to your fault and on your order, against her refusal and reluctance—if she cannot practice continence, she shall marry whom she prefers, only in the Lord.[67]

Second, various cases of fornication with different in-laws are taken up (sister-in-law, before and after marriage to a brother; step-daughter; step-mother; fiancée of son) and the solution is the same; penances for both sinners; permission for the respective husbands to divorce the culpable wife and to remarry; lifelong prohibition of remarriage for the wives.[68]

Fulbert († 1028), bishop of Chartres, had at Rheims been the pupil of Gerbert, later Sylvester II, one of the popes of the reform which culminated in Gregory VII. Fulbert founded in 990 his own school at Chartres, which soon became renowned. Among his letters is one directed to Robert, archbishop of Rouen, in which a husband is allowed to remarry when his wife enters religious life:

The impudence of Gualeramus, whom you have mentioned, has annoyed me beyond limits with his request for another marriage. However, I have continued to object by telling him that he is not permitted to usurp another wife as long as his first one is alive. Now finally he asked me, either cunningly or sincerely, whether I

66. Zhishman, *op. cit.,* p. 106. For the text of these canons, see Pitra, *Spicilegium Sollesmense,* vol. IV, 404, 406.
67. *PL* 140, 959.
68. *PL* 140, 966.

would either return to him his fugitive wife or, if she resists, ex-communicate her; otherwise, he said, I and she are making him commit adultery. The wife, having been summoned for this reason, replied to me that she would never return to him and, since she surely knew that her ways could never agree with the ways of Gualeramus, that she would sooner renounce the world and become a nun. . . .

Gualeramus often sends me messages asking permission to contract a new marriage, saying that she had turned away from him, that she had received his money, although not truly protesting. But I refuse him the permission *as long as* his wife has not become a nun or is not dead.[69]

From the contents of this letter it follows that Fulbert had no doubt that a new marriage could be permitted if the wife chose religious life voluntarily. Adultery was not alleged by the husband as ground for the separation. He had given the money for the dowry which she had requested but she refused to enter the convent, and Fulbert could see no possibility to permit a remarriage for him.

Alexius Studites, patriarch of Constantinople (1025–1043), is a witness of the definitely established practice of the Byzantine Church in respect to the remarriage of divorced persons. His decisions have been incorporated into the sources of canon law.

1. The priest who gives the marriage blessing to a woman divorced from her husband is not to be condemned if the man's conduct was the cause of separation.

2. Women divorced from husbands whose conduct was the cause of separation are blameless if they wish to marry [again], and so are the priests who give them the blessing of the union. The same rule applies to men.

3. The man who marries a woman divorced for adultery, whether he has himself been married before or not, is an adulterer, and must submit to the penance of adulterers.

4. The priest who gives his blessing on second marriages for

69. *PL* 141, 223.

those who have dissolved their marriage by mutual consent, which is not sanctioned by the laws, shall be deprived of his office.[70]

Theophylact (11th c.), archbishop of Ohrida, was one of the most famous of the medieval Greek exegetes. He explains the excepting clause of Matthew 19, 9, as follows: [71] "Jesus affirmed that he had not come to dissolve (*lyein*) the law of Moses, but only to correct and perfect it. According to the law of Moses, as understood by the Jewish interpreters, a husband could dismiss his wife for many reasons. Jesus corrected this by reducing it to one, namely, adultery, but he did not abolish the legal possibility of complete divorce and right of remarriage. In other words, he corrected divorce but did not abrogate it completely.

70. H. M. Lucknock, *The History of Marriage, Jewish and Christian, in Relation to Divorce and Certain Forbidden Degrees,* pp. 182 f.
71. *PG* 123, 197.

II.

THE WITNESS OF THE ROMAN PONTIFFS

St. Innocent I, pope from 401 to 417, has on several occasions made statements concerning the question of divorce and remarriage. In a letter to *Exuperius,* bishop of Toulouse in France, the Pope answers one of his questions: "Your diligence has asked also concerning those who by means of writ of divorce [*interveniente repudio*], have contracted another marriage. It is manifest that they are adulterers on both sides." [1] This seemed to many theologians a clear prohibition of any remarriage after any kind of divorce. However, in the light of so many instances of the Fathers permitting a new marriage to the husband after he had divorced his *adulterous* wife, it is not impossible that this is a prohibition of that divorce which is based only on mutual agreement.

In writing to *Victricius,* bishop of Rouen in France, Innocent I says: "In respect to all cases the rule is observed that whoever marries another man, while her husband is alive, must be held to be an adulteress, and must be granted no leave to do penance unless one of the men shall have died." [2] This too is in full agreement with the opinion of so many Fathers, that a wife can never enter a second marriage. No prohibition of remarriage for an aggrieved husband can be read into this statement.

The protracted absence of a spouse was declared insufficient as a ground for divorce in a letter to Probus. The facts of the case were these: Ursa had been taken away by the enemy. Her husband Fortunius then married Restituta. Ursa returned, and

1. *PL* 20, 400.
2. *PL* 20, 479.

the Pope judged that Fortunius must reestablish marriage with her because "Marriage with the second woman can in no way be legitimate if the former wife is alive and if she had not been ejected because of divorce." [3] The mere absence of a spouse cannot terminate a marriage, but it is implied that the second marriage would have been valid, and Fortunius could have stayed with Restituta, had Ursa been guilty of adultery.

St. Leo I, pope from 440 to 461, speaks in his letter to Nicetas, bishop of Aquileia, of wives whose husbands had been taken away as prisoners of war and who had in consequence married other men: "It is necessary that we affirm that the bond of lawful marriage be reestablished, and, after the harm had been undone which the hostilities had caused, that to each one be restored what lawfully belonged to him." [4] Inasmuch as adultery was not involved, the Pope's answer has nothing to say concerning this divorce ground.

St. Gregory I, pope from 590 to 604, has spoken out a few times about the dissolution of marriage. In his letter to Abbot Ursicus he opposes the entrance into religion of one marriage partner only, and insists that both or neither must embrace the religious state. The letter does not speak of divorce at all, whether it is permitted or forbidden. To the notary Hadrian, the Pope wrote: "Although the civil law provides that, for the sake of conversion [that is, for the purpose of choosing religious life], a marriage may be dissolved, though neither of the parties be unwilling, yet the divine law does not permit it to be done." [5]

Gregory again demands that both or neither enter religious life. Why should he oppose the frequently encountered example of one partner only entering a convent? From his reference

---

3. "Conventumque secundae mulieris, priori superstite, nec divortia eiecta, nullo pacto esse legitimum" (*PL* 20, 602).
4. *PL* 44, 1136.
5. *PL* 77, 833 and 1169.

to civil law we deduce the answer. Late Roman law permitted the spouses to dissolve the marriage by common agreement if one of them wished to enter religious life. The other spouse could remarry. It was a dissolution of a marriage beyond the only exception permitted by Christ, namely, adultery committed by the wife. This could be considered the reason why the Pope was against the choice of religious life by one spouse only.

In a letter to the patrician Teoktist the Pope mentions that the only reason for terminating a marriage is adultery on the part of the wife: "Truth Himself states: 'What God has joined together, let no man put asunder.' He also said: 'It is not permitted to dismiss the wife except because of fornication.' Who therefore will speak against this heavenly legislator?" [6]

St. Gregory II, pope from 715 to 731, is quoted as permitting divorce and remarriage. The text in question is found in Gratian's Decree [7] and says that when a wife cannot render the conjugal duties to her husband because of some ailment, he may remarry, if he so wishes, though he is supposed to support his first wife financially. It is not expressly said that the sickness mentioned existed prior to the marriage or appeared during the marriage. If she had the disease at the time of entering the marriage, it could have constituted the impediment of impotence, provided that it fell in this category, and this would render the marriage invalid by divine law. If the disease appeared later, then it would not influence the validity of the marriage at all, and, according to present practice, would not permit divorce and remarriage to the husband.

Gratian understood the passage in the second meaning, that is, that the Pope permitted dissolution of a sacramental marriage and the entering of a new marriage; of this Gratian observed: "This [decision] of Gregory is to be considered entirely opposed to the sacred canons, and even to the teaching of the Gospel and the apostles."

6. Rouët de Journel, *Enchiridion Patristicum,* 2297 *in fine.*
7. *PL* 89, 525. See also *PL* 99, 1153.

We find the decree ascribed to St. Gregory II in perfect agreement with the practice of the entire Church of his time, in the East, in and outside the Byzantine Empire, as well as in the West, especially in the Kingdom of the Franks.

St. Zachary, pope from 741 to 752, a Greek, wrote in a letter of January 5, 747, addressed to Pepin and the Frankish notables: "If any layman shall put away his own wife and marry another, or if he shall marry a woman who has been put away by another man, let him be deprived of communion." [8] While this text is often seen as a proof for the Pope's assumed belief in the indissolubility of marriage, it can be much better explained as a prohibition of unjustified divorce and remarriage. The grounds for divorce recognized at that time were adultery and entrance into religious life. The adulterous wife was forever forbidden to remarry, while the husband could not commit adultery in a legal sense. The Pope speaks only of unjustified divorce.

The reason why there is a special mention of "layman" may be that second marriages after a justified divorce were permitted to husbands with the exception of clerics, to whom a second marriage was forbidden by St. Paul even after the death of the wife. This is still the law for Eastern Catholic and Orthodox deacons and priests.

St. Zachary, coming from the Eastern Church, could not have ignored the practice of the entire Christian Orient, and we cannot assume that he wished to uphold in the Western Church a matrimonial discipline different from that of the Byzantine Empire. In our opinion, therefore, this document ought to be considered a genuine affirmation of divorce and remarriage.

Another document is also ascribed to St. Zachary, but since it permits remarriage during the lifetime of the first spouse and does not have the usual form of papal declarations, it has been considered spurious. Being quoted in Gratian's Decree, it

8. *Monumenta Germanica Historica Epist. III Epist. Merov. et Karolini aevi,* p. 482.

is certainly a witness to the persuasion of Gratian that in preceding centuries divorce was permitted:

You have slept with the sister of your wife? If you did this, you shall have neither of them, and if she who was your wife was not aware of the crime, if she does not wish to be continent, she may marry in the Lord whomever she prefers. You, however, and the adulteress shall remain without hope of marriage, and for as long as you both live, you shall do penance according to the instruction of the priest.[9]

This has been explained as if it were the case of a man having intercourse with his *future* sister-in-law before his marriage. In that way it would have been a diriment impediment. But how could the Pope then call the sister-in-law an adulteress if the man was not yet married? A more plausible explanation would be that this form of incest gave the innocent wife a ground for divorce and right of remarriage, while it constituted a perpetual impediment between the culprits.

Stephen II, pope from 752 to 757, issued on his journey to Pepin the Short in 754 instructions in various matters among which are several relative to marriage problems.

When in a marriage a spouse becomes incapable of sexual intercourse or afflicted with some other infirmity, separation is not permitted, except because of mental disorder or leprosy. It is not stated whether the nonafflicted spouse can remarry.[10]

The next reply refers to a marriage between a man and a slave girl (*ancilla*), whom he leaves to marry a free woman. If he abandons the latter, he can return to the former if she is not married to somebody else. Otherwise, he cannot contract a new marriage as long as his second wife, a free woman (*ingenua*), is alive.[11] This seems to imply that the marriage with a slave girl could be totally dissolved but not the valid marriage with a free woman. This example is different from that

9. *PL* 89, 959.
10. *PL* 89, 1024.
11. *Ibid.*

mentioned in canon 1083 #2, n. 2, of the *CIC,* when a marriage partner considered the other to be a free person while he or she was a slave. In the above case decided by Pope Stephen II, the husband was well aware of the legal status of the bride, that is, that she was not a free woman.

A council held in Rome during the reign of Stephen II enacted as canon 36:

Nobody is permitted, except on the ground of fornication, to abandon a wife with whom he had intercourse and then to marry another; if it happened otherwise, it is proper that the transgressor rejoin the first marriage. If, however, the man and the wife agree among themselves that they would separate only for the sake of entering religious life, this shall not be done without the knowledge of the bishop, in order that they may be questioned each in a determined place. For if the wife or husband is opposed the marriage is not dissolved for such a cause.[12]

Stephen III, pope between 768 and 772, was questioned whether a husband could remarry who had repudiated his wife: "If a wife was repudiated by her husband, is it permitted to the husband to take another if the former is still alive?" [13] He answers by referring to the letter of Innocent I to Exuperius of Toulouse.[14] This letter seems to forbid any divorce but ought probably to be understood as referring solely to the question of arbitrariness and injustice on the part of the husband in respect to the wife. No reference or exclusion of divorce because of adultery is mentioned, which would have to be expected if the pope wished to state his disapproval of the contemporary canonical order.

Eugene II, pope from 824 to 827, held a council of 62 bishops in 826 in Rome, at which a canon 36 was passed. It is a repetition of the canon 36 promulgated under Stephen II which prohibits divorce except in case of adultery and entrance

12. *Monumenta,* p. 493.
13. *Ibid.,* pp. 558–567; 713–715.
14. See note 1.

into religious life. It is significant that the legal concepts had not yet changed.[15]

St. Leo IV (847–855) assembled an important synod in Rome in 853, which in the matter of divorce repeated what was said at the council of 826 under Eugene II, and which had reenacted the laws passed by the council of 754 under Stephen II.[16] Since these statutes permit divorce in various instances, it cannot be asserted that the popes condemned it. However, this is sometimes explained as a mere toleration of an abuse which the Roman pontiffs could not abolish at that time. To this one could reply that such a silence must have been regarded by other parts of the Church as tacit approval, in accordance with the axiom: *Qui tacet consentire videtur* (He who is silent can be presumed to consent).

John VIII, pope from 872 to 882, has in his letter to Edred, archbishop of Canterbury (877), a clear prohibition for either spouse to remarry after divorce, even if adultery had been committed:

But to those who, as you state, desert their own wives contrary to the command of the Lord, we order that neither shall a husband leave his wife nor a wife her husband except because of fornication. If he [she] for this [reason] left, he [she] shall remain unmarried, or they shall mutually become reconciled, since the Lord says: "What God has joined, let man not separate"; and therefore, as a man cannot desert the first wife with whom he was united in lawful matrimony, so also it is not permitted for any reason whatever to take another wife while the former is alive. If he did that and does not endeavor to make satisfactory amend, he shall remain separated from ecclesiastical participation.[17]

Celestine III (1191–1198) confirmed the decision of a di-

15. D. Palmieri, *Tractatus de matrimonio christiano,* p. 388; *Monumenta: Leges,* IV, p. 545; *Monumenta, Capitularia,* I, p. 332.
16. Mansi, vol. XIV, pp. 882–1032; *Monumenta,* VII, pp. 1912–1928.
17. *PL* 126, 746, and *Monumenta,* vol. VII, pp. 1912–1928.

ocesan official, who had permitted a Catholic woman to contract a new marriage after her Catholic husband had become an apostate from the faith. However, his successor Innocent III (1198–1216) disavowed heresy or apostasy as a ground for divorce in a reply to the bishop of Ferrara, "in spite that a certain predecessor of Ours apparently thought differently." [18]

18. *Decretales,* chap. VII, IV, p. 19.

III.

THE WITNESS OF THE SYNODS

The Apostolic Canons is a collection of ecclesiastical statutes dating from the fourth century. Canon 48 says: "If a layman dismisses his wife and marries another, or if he takes a wife dismissed by another, he shall be deprived of communion." [1] This probably refers to unjustified repudiation of a wife, that is, one who was not charged with adultery. The mentioning of the layman was necessary only if a distinction from the clergy was intended. A deacon, priest, or bishop could only be "one wife's husband," and they were therefore prevented from contracting a second marriage, while laymen could remarry either after the death of their wives or after a justified divorce because of adultery on the part of the wife.

Deprivation of communion was a vindicative punishment, that is, inflicted as a penance for a second marriage after legal divorce, to last a certain number of years. The penalized act itself was not considered invalid, but it was felt that a spiritual balance should be restored by counterposing to the second marriage after divorce a corresponding penance.

Elvira in Spain was the place of a council held soon after 300 under the presidency of Hosius of Cordoba. The 81 canons are a witness to ecclesiastical life in the Iberian Peninsula at that time.

Canon 8: Also women who have left their husbands with no preceding cause and have married other men, shall not receive communion even at the end. [2]

1. Pitra, *Iuris ecclesiastici Graecorum historia et monumenta,* vol. I, p. 24.
2. Mansi, vol. II, p. 7.

Canon 9: Let a believing woman who has left a believing adulterous husband and is marrying another be prohibited from marrying; if she has married, let her not receive communion until the man she has left shall have departed this life, unless perhaps urgency of illness should compel to grant it.[3]

These are two of the numerous contemporary texts which treat of the remarriage of divorced women. Catholic theologians have interpreted this as a sign that the indissolubility of marriage was already an established principle in Spain. They have not tried to explain why all these documents speak only of the remarriage of the wife and never, or seldom and then without the necessary clarity, of the remarriage of husbands. The most obvious explanation concerns the difference in the legal rights of husbands and wives. A husband could remarry if his wife committed adultery, while a wife could never remarry even if she was innocent and the husband guilty of misconduct. These principles were so well established in the mind of the early Church that they were taken for granted and very rarely mentioned. What was troubling the bishops was the inequality of the wives who could not remarry even if the husband was guilty of adultery. However, the council affirmed the law of Matthew 19, 9 (*excepta fornicationis causa*), which speaks only of an adultery of the wife, and gives right to remarriage only to the husband.

Arles was the place of a council held in 314, which issued 22 canons, among which is the following:

Canon 10: To those who apprehend their wives in adultery, who are young believers, and are [not] prohibited from marrying, if possible the counsel is given that they should not take others as long as their own wives are alive, in spite of the face that the wives are adulterous.[4]

3. *PL* 84, 303.
4. "De his qui coniuges suas in adulterio depraehendunt, et idem sunt adulescentes fideles et (non) prohibentur nubere, placuit ut, quantum possit, consilium eis detur ne alias uxores, viventibus etiam uxoribus suis licet adulteris, accipiant" (*Corpus Christianorum, Series Latina. CXLVIII. Concilia Galliae,* p. 11).

In some manuscripts the particle "not" is missing, but the Codex Herovallianus (Heronville) supplies it. However, even without it the meaning would be clear, because otherwise why should they be *counseled* not to marry if they could not marry anyway? Jacques Petit, who in the seventeenth century prepared an edition of the acts of the council, quotes St. Augustine's opinion on this decision: "The Fathers of this very renowned council do not inflict any punishment but give only a counsel. Thus, the Fathers say that the matter is not forbidden."

The *Council of Carthage* was convened in 407 under the presidency of Aurelius, bishop of Carthage, and decreed in Canon 105:

In respect to those who dismiss their wives or husbands: that they shall remain so. In view of the discipline of the Gospel and of the Apostle, neither he who was deserted by his wife, nor she who was dismissed by the husband, shall join up with another; but they shall either remain so or shall become reconciled; if they should disregard this, they shall be compelled to penance.[5]

This seemingly unconditional prohibition of any divorce, even on the ground of adultery, probably referred to a separation in which the wife could not be charged with adultery. Because of the practice of other Churches to permit in such instances total divorce to an aggrieved husband with the right to marry again, the bishops could have been expected to exclude even this possibility, of which they must have been aware, if they actually intended to exclude it.

The second council held at *Milevis* in northern Africa in 416 under the presidency of Aurelius, bishop of Carthage, was attended also by St. Augustine of Hippo. It decreed:

Canon 17: In accordance with evangelical and apostolic discipline, neither the husband dismissed by the wife, nor the wife dismissed by the husband shall marry another spouse; but they shall remain in that state and shall be reconciled with each other,

5. Labbe, *Sacrosancta Concilia ad regiam editionem executa,* vol. II, pp. 1113 ff.; *Palmieri, op. cit.,* p. 332.

and if they disregard this, they shall be compelled to do penance. An imperial law shall be requested and promulgated in this matter.[6]

At first reading, this canon appears to prohibit remarriage of divorced spouses. However, the reference to the teaching of the Gospel and St. Paul probably means that only divorce by mutual consent or for some other reason, but excepting adultery, was here understood. Since husbands were permitted to remarry if they divorced an adulterous wife, and this was considered in conformity with the Gospel (Mt. 19, 9), the bishops would have expressly excluded this too, had they ever wished to enact an exclusion of every absolute divorce. Of course, it could be argued that adultery of wives was a rather rare occurrence, and marital infidelity of the husband did not constitute legal adultery, and that this was the reason why the Fathers of the Council ignored it. Also, the reference to imperial laws to include also this prohibition are an indication that something which civil law did not forbid, namely, divorce by mutual consent, should now become prohibited. Joseph Zhishman, who knows this canon according to another source as the 107th of Carthage, thinks that the reference to an imperial law which is to be proposed by the Council Fathers can be explained in one way only: namely, that divorce and remarriage would then be permitted; in the meantime, they shall either be reconciled or shall live separately. If they disobeyed and remarried, they are subject to penance, as long as no imperial law has sanctioned remarriage.[7]

Angers was the see occupied by Thalasius, bishop since 453, at which time a council was held there. Thalasius left a brief but valuable compendium of canon law, consisting of decisions

---

6. "Placuit ut secundam evangelicam at apostolicam disciplinam, neque dimissus ab uxore, nec dimissa a marito alteri coniungantur; sed ita maneant aut sibimet reconcilientur, quod si contempserint, ad poenitentiam redigantur. In qua causa legem imperialem petendam est promulgari" (Mansi, vol. IV, p. 331; Labbe, vol. IV, p. 331).

7. *Op. cit.,* p. 112.

of various councils convoked in the dioceses of the ecclesiastical province of Tours in France. At the Council of 453 this canon was passed: "Also, those who abuse the name of marriage by [joining] the wives of others while their husbands are still alive, shall be treated as strangers." [8] The Council here considered solely the remarriage of wives and declared it forbidden, abstracting entirely from inquiring whether they were innocent or culpable of adultery. Husbands who had separated because of adultery could validly remarry, and no special mention was deemed necessary of a rule which was applied everywhere.

The so-called *Synod of St. Patrick* (460?) decreed:
XXVI. Likewise, a man is not permitted to dismiss his wife except because of fornication, as if he would say: for this reason. Therefore, if he takes another just as after the death of the former [wife], they do not prohibit it.[9]

Vannes (Vaneticum) was the site of several councils of the early French Church. One of them, held in 461 or 465, enacted this canon:
2. In respect also of those who have deserted their wives, as it is said in the Gospel "except for fornication," and have without proving adultery married others, we decree that they are likewise to be barred from communion, lest the sins passed over by our indulgence should attract others to the licentiousness of error.[10]

There is no doubt that the bishops of Gaul at that time considered adultery of the wife a valid and sufficient reason for divorce. Since, however, some husbands remarried without having furnished proof of such adultery, it was assumed that they repudiated their wives for other, non-canonical reasons.

8. *Corpus Christianorum*, p. 138.
9. *PL* 53, 822.
10. "2. Eos quoque, qui relictis uxoribus suis, sicut in evangelio dicitur 'excepta causa fornicationis,' sine adulterii probatione alias duxerint, statuimus a communione similiter arcendos, ne per indulgentiam nostram praetermissa peccata alios ad licentiam erroris invitent" (*Corpus Christianorum*, p. 152).

Agde (Agatha), now in the diocese of Montpellier, was the seat of a bishop since the beginning of the fifth century. A council was held there in 506 under the presidency of St. Caesarius of Arles. One of the canons treats of marriage dissolutions:

However, those laymen who dissolve married life or have already dissolved it, committing a serious sin, and do not furnish any probable reasons for the separation, dissolving for this reason their marriages in order to attempt unlawful or forbidden ones—if they, before having submitted the ground for separation to the provincial bishops and before the wives have been found guilty by the court, had driven them away, then such husbands shall be excluded from the ecclesiastical communion and from the holy assembly of the people, because they defile faith and marriage.[11]

The synod reserves to the council of the bishops of the ecclesiastical province the right to judge cases of marriage dissolutions. Those are to be excommunicated who remarry before the bishops had an opportunity to investigate and confirm the guilt of the wife, that is, adultery on her part. Divorce and remarriage as such are not forbidden, provided there is a sufficient reason, which was only adultery on the part of wives, and official confirmation by an ecclesiastical court. It is significant that again solely the misconduct of wives is considered, since that of husbands did not entitle either the wife or the husband to a divorce. The specific mention of "laymen" has already been explained.

Orleans was the site of a synod gathered in 533 as a national council under King Childebert. It forbade divorce under pretext of a sickness or infirmity which appeared subsequent to the marriage contract. It was natural to condemn this great injustice of abandoning a spouse because of a disease contracted during the marriage:

11. Marriages which have been [lawfully] contracted shall not be dissolved on account of a subsequent infirmity, notwithstand-

11. *Ibid.,* p. 204.

ing any intention to the contrary. If some spouses should nevertheless do it, they shall know that they will be deprived of
communion.[12]

If the bishops of the Frankish Church had been convinced
that any divorce was forbidden, they would have spoken of
the general prohibition, perhaps including the particular ground
of infirmity. The silence of the synod permits one to draw the
conclusion that absolute divorce was possible for another
reason than that mentioned in the canon, namely, adultery.

Hereford was the site of a provincial synod held in 673. The
canons adopted are a witness to the discipline current at that
time in England.

Every priest shall publicly admonish the people to abstain from
unlawful marriages, for a lawful marriage can by no means be
separated in accordance with the command of the Lord, except
by reason of fornication, or except by mutual consent and this
because of the service of God.[13]

Two grounds for the ending of a marriage are sanctioned in
this canon: adultery and entrance into a convent, the latter
with the consent of the other spouse. Nothing is said about the
right of remarriage, but from the contemporary usage, especially across the Channel in France, it can be concluded that it
was permitted in England too; otherwise, it would have been
strange for the synod not expressly to forbid it.

Nobody shall desert his own wife except, as the holy Gospel
teaches, because of fornication. But if any man has expelled his
own wife, who was joined to him in lawful marriage, if he wishes
to be truly a Christian, he shall not join another [woman] but
shall remain so, or he shall be reconciled to his own wife.[14]

Some explain this as a prohibition of remarriage and point
to the discrepancy between the contents of this canon and the
legislation elsewhere ascribed to Theodore of Canterbury who

12. Mansi, vol. VIII, p. 837.
13. Labbe, vol. IX, p. 46.
14. Lucknock, *op. cit.*, pp. 199–201.

188

was the president of this synod. Especially do the Penitentials ascribed to the archbishop permit divorce and remarriage because of adultery. However, this canon speaks of two different cases. The first concerns divorce because of the adultery of the wife. The second one treats of the instance when a husband has expelled his wife on other grounds.

Hibernia Secunda, or Secunda Sancti Patricii, was a council held towards the close of the seventh century, although the acts purport to go back to St. Patrick. " 'The husband is not permitted to dismiss the wife except because of fornication,' as if He says: 'because of this reason.' Therefore, if he remarries another wife, just as if after the death of the first wife, they do not veto it." [15] Adultery is said to be equal to death and thus to produce the same legal effect, dissolution of the marriage bond. Remarriage is therefore not forbidden.

Soissons in France was the site of a council celebrated in 744. *Canon 9.* Similarly, we decree that no layman shall take as wife a woman consecrated to God, nor a relative of his, nor shall during the lifetime of a husband another man take his wife, nor shall the wife during the lifetime of her husband take another man, because the husband must not dismiss his woman except because he apprehended her in fornication.[16]

The only ground for divorce was adultery of the wife, which gave the husband, but not the wife, the right to remarriage. This is supported by reference to Matthew 19, 9. Significant is the addition of the requirement that the wife must have been *apprehended;* in other words, rumor or the accusation of the husband alone was not sufficient.

Verberie in France was in 752 the site of a council which enacted several canons on marriage law. They are listed in

15. Hardouin, *Conciliorum collectio regia maxima,* vol. I, col. 1786.
16. *PL* 89, 826.

various canonical collections of the next centuries, as in that of Regino of Prüm († 915) and of Burchard of Worms († 1025). The following canons are of interest here:

Canon 2. If anyone stays with his step-daughter, he cannot have either the mother or her daughter, nor can he nor she at any time marry anybody else. The wife, however, if she so wishes, and if she cannot be continent, after she has found out that her daughter was in adultery with the husband shall not have carnal intercourse with him, and if she does not wish to abstain voluntarily, can marry another.[17]

Canon 5. If a wife seeks in conspiracy with others to procure the death of her husband and her husband killed the man in defending himself, and he can prove this, this husband, as it appears to us, can dismiss the wife, and if he wishes take another. The ambushing wife herself shall be subjected to penance and shall remain without hope of marriage.[18]

Canon 9. If a man, compelled by unavoidable necessity, has fled to another duchy or province, or if he had followed his lord, to whom he had promised faith and faithfulness and therefore cannot refuse, and his wife, although she could and is able, will not go with him because of her love for her parents or relatives, she shall forever stay unmarried as long as the husband whom she did not follow lives. But he who remains in another country because of a compelling need, if he has no hope of ever returning to his home country, and if he cannot live continently, may take another wife, after having done penance.[19]

Canon 10. If the son slept with his step-mother, the wife of his father, neither he [the son] nor she can attain marriage. But that man [the father], if he wishes, can have another wife; but it is better to abstain.[20]

Canon 11. If anyone slept with his step-daughter, he can be

17. Hardouin, vol. III, col. 1990.
18. *PL* 132, 307.
19. *PL* 99, 1156; 132, 308.
20. Hardouin, *loc. cit.*

subject to the same sentence; and with the sister of his wife, he can be treated in the same way.[21]

Canon 18. He who stays with a cousin of his wife, shall be deprived of his own wife, and shall not have any other; that woman whom he had may do what she wishes. This the Church does not accept.[22]

Canon 21. He who permitted his wife to accept the veil, may not accept another wife.[23]

According to the Council of Verberie the following reasons permit divorce and remarriage:

(1) Adultery, especially with blood relations and affines.

(2) Machinations against the life of the spouse.

(3) Refusal of a wife to follow her husband in a justifiable emigration to another country permits the husband to remarry there.

The permission granted to a wife to enter a convent does not entitle the husband to remarry. This is not consonant with other contemporary statutes, and might have been indicated by the occurrence of cases of wives who chose the religious life because so pressured or forced by their husbands.

Compiegne in France was the site of a council held in 757. It is a witness of a liberal policy of Church and state in respect to divorce and remarriage. Canon 13 permits a spouse to enter religious life with the consent of the other, and allows the one who remains in the world to remarry. To this is added that *"Georgius consensit,"* [24] namely, that the papal legate George, bishop of Ostia, approved of it.

Canon 6. A Frank accepted from his lord a fief in another province, and he took with him his vassal. When then later the lord died, the aforementioned vassal continued to stay there. An-

---

21. *Ibid.*
22. *Ibid.*
23. *PL* 132, 309.
24. *PL* 99, 1153; Labbe, vol. VIII, p. 452.

191

other man accepted then the same fief, and in order to secure the service of the same vassal, he gave him a wife from the same fief, and he had her for a certain time. But since this lord mistreated him, he dismissed the wife and returned to the family of his late lord, and took another wife. It was decided that he may have her whom he took later.[25]

Canon 19 (or 16) permits the dissolution of a marriage if the husband has contracted leprosy, and allows the wife to remarry, with the consent of the leper husband.[26]

Canon 8. If a man has a legitimate wife and his brother commits adultery with her, that brother and that woman who committed adultery shall never have [a right to] marriage. He whose wife she was, if he wishes, is entitled to take another wife.[27]

Friuli, a region of northern Italy, was the place of a council held in 791. No other council, pope, or ecclesiastical writer of the first millennium has ever so clearly and definitely expressed the doctrine of absolute indissolubility of Christian marriage:

Chapter 10. Likewise, it pleased [to decree] that it shall not be permitted to the husband, the matrimonial bond having been dissolved because of fornication, to take another wife as long as the adulterous spouse is alive, despite the fact that she is adulterous . . . Therefore, one is given patently to understand: the husband is not permitted, nor can he without impunity contract a second marriage as long as the adulterous wife lives.[28]

This explicit and apodictic statement suggests that the common practice and the doctrinal justification at the time of the council was permissive in respect to remarriage of husbands of adulterous wives, and that this had to be opposed in clear and unambiguous language.

Eminent among the numerous collections called *capitularia* is the *Capitulary of Charlemagne,* the first part of the collec-

25. *PL* 132, 309.
26. Labbe, vol. VIII, p. 453.
27. *PL* 99, 1151; Hardouin, vol. III, p. 206.
28. Mansi, vol. XIII, p. 849; Hardouin, vol. IV, col. 859; Labbe, vol. IX, p. 46.

tion prepared in 827 by Ansegisus, abbot of Fontanelle. Several *capitula* refer to divorce. One is a repetition of earlier synodal enactments preceding the time of Charlemagne, and permits a husband to take another wife if his first wife has committed adultery with his brother.[29] It is significant that in spite of the absolute prohibition of divorce by a few councils of his times, the learned St. Ansegisus included this law in his collection, apparently because he considered it a valid statute.

The council of *Paris* of 829 was a regional synod gathered from the four ecclesiastical provinces of Rheims, Sens, Tours, and Rouen. It enacted as law "That those who dismiss their wives on the ground of fornication and take others shall be known as adulterers by the law of the Lord." [30]

We find here the principle of total exclusion of any divorce which was one of the postulates of the great reform beginning in the ninth century and culminating in the eleventh under Gregory VII and in the thirteenth under Innocent III.

The council of *Nantes* (875) in France enacted this statute:
Canon 12. If anyone's wife committed adultery, and this has been discovered by the husband and made public, he shall dismiss the wife if he wishes, because of fornication. But she shall do public penance for seven years. Her husband, however, cannot take another wife by any means as long as she lives.[31]

This too is a witness to the new spirit pervading the Church in the West which in the next two centuries also evolved a stern discipline with regard to celibacy of the clergy and the lay investiture of clerics.

The council of *Tribur* (Trebur) in Germany (895) decreed:

29. The text is identical with that of canon 8 of Compiegne (see *Capitularia Regum Francorum*, col. 829).
30. "Quod hi, qui causa fornicationis dimissis uxoribus suis, alias ducunt, Domini sententia adulteri esse notentur" (Hardouin, vol. IV, col. 1353).
31. *PL* 132, 309; Hardouin, vol. VI, col. 460.

"46. The husband shall in no way take another wife as long as she herself [the adulterous one] is alive." [32]

The Penitential of Theodore cites as canon 41 of the same council a canon which indicates that the prohibition of divorce was not absolute:

41. If someone took a legitimate wife, and is hindered by a domestic infirmity from fulfilling his marital duty with her, and his brother, under the influence of the devil, falls in love with her and secretly humiliates her, and violates her, they shall be completely separated, and this woman henceforth shall not be touched by anyone. Therefore, the marriage which had been legitimate has become defiled because of this pollution by the brother. What had been lawful has become unlawful. Also, as Jerome said: The wife of two brothers shall not mount the nuptial bed; if she mounts it, she commits adultery. However, because human nature is inclined to fall, it shall be fortified by some means to be able to withstand. Therefore, the bishop, having consideration of the feebleness of their minds, after the penance had been performed according to his instruction, shall let them be consoled with a lawful marriage if they cannot be continent, lest they sink into the mud while they are expected to be raised to higher things.[33]

This is often explained as referring to a marriage which was invalid because of impotence on the part of the husband, or to a marriage which has not been consummated. However, from the title given to the whole chapter in the Penitential of Theodore and from the other statutes cited in the Penitential under the same heading (Burchard, Lib. XIX, cap. 4; Council of Compiegne, can. 8), it is clear that the collector of the Penitential referred it to any marriage in which an incestuous relationship had developed between the wife and her brother-in-law, and that he permitted remarriage to both. Also, the fact that this canon was not taken over into the subsequent collection of canons of this council seems to indicate that the omission was considered necessary, since in the meantime the

32. "Maritus, quamdiu ipsa (adultera) vivit, nullo modo alteram ducat" (Hardouin, vol. VII, col. 454; Mansi, vol. XVIII, p. 152).
33. *PL* 99, 1151.

doctrine which excluded any divorce and remarriage had become prevalent, and the collector rightly understood this canon as permitting it.

The synod of *Ingelheim* in Germany, held in 948, is another witness to a change in the practice of the Western Church:

Canon 9. We confirm that it is permitted to every Christian to dismiss a wife only because of fornication, by virtue of the authority of the Gospel, and the legislation of the sacred canons, but we do not approve by any means that he takes another wife while the first one is alive.[34]

The Laws of the Northumbrian Priests date from the middle of the tenth century, and their wording, seemingly opposing remarriage, can be understood only if we assume that divorce because of adultery was tacitly permitted. "Anathema upon any one in holy orders who should divorce a wife and marry again." Clergy, even if lawfully married, could not remarry after ordination, not even after the death of the wife. In respect to laymen it was decreed that "if any one should divorce his lawful wife and marry another, he should want God's mercy, unless he made satisfaction . . ."[35] The distinction between the married clergy and the laity can be understood only if the laity were permitted to remarry after a justified divorce and the clergy were not.

34. Quoted in P. Daudet, *L'établissement de la compétence de l'Eglise en matière de divorce et de consanguinité (France, Xième-XIIIème siècles)*, p. 19.
35. Lucknock, *op. cit.*, p. 203.

IV.

PENITENTIALS AND FORMULARIES

Poenitentiale Vinniai (Finnian), probably from around 550, is of Irish provenance and contains a clear exclusion of re-marriage even in case of adultery of the wife: "42. If the wife of a man has committted fornication and lives with another man, he ought not to take another wife as long as his wife is alive." [1]

Formularies of Angers is a collection of examples of private and public documents—some going back to the sixth century but the greater part from the seventh—which witness to a very liberal marriage discipline.

56. Form for Dissolving Marriage.

To my Lord, not the sweetest, but the bitterest and most tem-peramental spouse N. Whereas it is not unknown how because of dislike and divine prohibition we cannot stay together, it is thus befitting in the sight of good men that we must free the reins of each other, which we hereby do. Whenever my husband shall wish to take a wife, he shall have the free power to do so . . . Likewise also he agrees that whenever the aforesaid wife herself wishes to take another husband, she has the free power to do so . . . [2]

Another form for dissolving marriage from the same time but of unknown source is as follows:

Since between N. and his wife N. no charity according to God but discord reigns between them, and because likewise they cannot by any means uphold it, it has pleased both to agree that they ought to be separated from this partnership, which they hereby have done. Therefore, they have decided by mutual

1. "42. Si alicuius uxor fornicata fuerit et habitet cum alio viro, non opportet adducere uxorem aliam, quamdiu fuerit uxor eius viva".
2. *PL* 87, 854.

agreement that these letters should be written and signed, in order that each of them have permission either to chose the service of God in a monastery or to contract marriage, and that there is no need of a request or that there is no obligation to have anything beyond what was promised . . .[3]

Poenitentiale Cummeani, from around 660, is ascribed to one of the several Irish saints of that name. The following rule, which is also found in Theodore of Canterbury's Penitential, refers to divorce:

30. However, one spouse can grant permission to the other to enter the service of God in a monastery and he himself can remarry. If he [she] was in his first marriage, this is not canonical according to the Greek usage only; but if in his second, he [she] is not permitted to contract a third marriage during the lifetime of the husband of wife.[4]

Formularies of Marculf is a canonical collection, the author of which is the monk Marculf, who towards the end of the seventh century collected examples of public and private documents from France. They encompass also marriage law, as it was applied at the time of the Merovingians. Divorce and marriage with other partners was permitted to both spouses even on the ground of incompatibility and mutual consent.[5]

Penitential of Theodore, archbishop of Canterbury, of whom we spoke in an earlier chapter, was one of the most influential canonical collections of this kind in Western Europe during the last three centuries of the first millennium. We present here several excerpts which need little interpretation. They sometimes contradict themselves, no doubt a sign that they come from different sources:

XIII. 5. If a slaveman or a slavewoman have been joined in matrimony by the master of both, and later the slaveman, or the slavewoman, has become free, if he or she who remains in

3. *PL* 87, 894.
4. Schmitz, *op. cit.,* vol. I, p. 649.
5. *PL* 87, 746.

slavery cannot be bought free, the free spouse is permitted to marry a free person.[6]

He who dismissed his wife and married another shall do strict penance for seven years or a lighter one for fifteen.[7]

31. To him whose wife has been taken away by the enemy, if he cannot retrieve her, it is permitted to take another wife; it is better to do this than to commit fornication. And if she returns later, he is not obliged to receive her back if he has another. She herself may take another husband if she had only one before.[8]

61. If the wife was taken away into captivity by force, he can take another wife after one year." [9]

140. The layman whose wife left him can, with the consent of the bishop, take another after two years.[10]

A layman could do this, while a clergyman was forbidden to marry again according to St. Paul's ordinance. If the clergy had been celibate at the time, no reference to them would have been necessary and no distinction between them and laymen would have been needed in such instances.

24. If that wife again returns to him afterwards, he is not obliged to receive her back if she had another man, but she can take another husband if she had only one before. The same rule applies to slaves from oversea.

20. If a wife that was abducted by force into captivity cannot be redeemed, he may take another after one year.

6. Schmitz, op. cit., vol. I, p. 548.
7. Ibid., p. 502.
8. "Cui uxorem hostis abstulerit, et non potest repetere eam, licet ei aliam accipere; melius est quam fornicari. Nam si postea redeat uxor, non debet recipere eam, si aliam habeat. Ipsa accipiet alterum virum, si unum ante habuit."
9. "Mulier si in captivitatem per vim ducta est, post annum aliam accipere potest."
10. "Laicus a quo recessit mulier, cum consensu episcopi post duos annos aliam accipiat."

198

21. Likewise, if she was taken into captivity, the husband shall wait five years, and similarly the wife, if this should happen to the husband.

22. If, therefore, the husband took another wife, he shall take back the former wife if she returns from captivity, and the second one he shall dismiss; likewise, she shall do as we said above, if this should happen to the husband.

19. If a wife left her husband out of disrespect for him, and refuses to return and be reconciled with the husband, it will be permitted to him to take, with the consent of the bishop another wife after five years.

143. If somebody's wife has committed fornication, it is permitted to dismiss her and to take another.

II. 5. #5. If the wife of anyone commits fornication, it is allowed to dismiss her and to take another; that is, if the husband dismisses his wife because of fornication, and she was his first wife, he is permitted to take another wife; while she, if she agrees to do penance for her sins, may take another man after five years.

Roman Penitential is the name given to a collection of norms which Halitgarius, Bishop of Cambrai in France (817–839), professes to have assembled from material found in the archives of the Roman Church (*de scrinio Romanae Ecclesiae*). One of the norms reads: "If anyone has a legitimate wife and dismisses her and takes another, she whom he took is not his." [11] This is an unqualified statement, not making any reference to adultery, which at that time was generally a valid divorce ground and gave right to marry again. It could be argued that this Roman Penitential belongs to the period of the Carolingian reform when there was a tendency to restrict

11. "Si quis legitimam uxorem habens dimiserit illam, et aliam duxit, illa quam duxit non est illius" (Schmitz, *op. cit.*, p. 487).

199

and exclude total divorce. However, just for that reason we would expect a clear reference and an emphatic condemnation of the permission for remarriage, and also a mention of justified separation of the spouses, if not a divorce. The absence of such a reference leads us to assume that this statute refers solely to divorce unjustified by adultery on the part of the wife.

Poenitentiale Vallicenum I, from the end of the tenth century, quotes a decree of one of the popes named Leo:

41. If anyone's wife was carried away by the enemy and he cannot redeem her, he is allowed to take another, and if she later returns, she also shall take another man; this applies also to the slaves from oversea.[12]

Poenitentiale Laurentianum is the name given by H. J. Schmitz to a collection of penitential rules found in a manuscript of the thirteenth century. Among these is the following excerpt from the Corrector of Burchard, bishop of Worms (1042):

48. It is allowed to dismiss a wife who is guilty of adultery, and if the husband or the wife left for a distant country, or if they have fallen victims of a strong detachment of pagans or of the wicked rule of a malicious Christian, he or she shall be expected for five years, and afterwards he or she may do what is necessary.[13]

No special exegesis is necessary for one to recognize here a clear permission for either spouse to remarry if the other was voluntarily or against his wish separated for five years. Nothing is said in respect to the possibility that the spouse might return later.

It is certainly significant that such a statute was inserted in the most important collection of that time, namely, at the beginning of the eleventh century, and that somebody found it worthwhile to transcribe it two hundred years later.

12. *Ibid.,* p. 487.
13. *Ibid.,* p. 789.

V.

THE TREATMENT
OF ROYALTY

CHURCH history has recorded several contests between popes and monarchs in which the object of the difference was the divorce attempted by the princes against the opposition of the Church. Theologians make use of these instances to prove that the popes were defending the indissolubility of marriage against encroachment of the secular power. While it is not maintained that these popes were not convinced that Christian marriage is absolutely indissoluble, we deny that from these examples a proof of indissolubility can be forged.

We refer to the following incidents: [1]

(1) Pepin the Short (714–768), King of the Franks, repudiated Bertranda in order to marry Angla, but Pope Zachary protested.

(2) Charlemagne repudiated Hilmitrude in order to marry Desiderata, daughter of the King of the Langobards. Pope Stephen III protested. Desiderata was dismissed in 770.

(3) Lothair II, King of Lotharingia, in 857 repudiated his wife Theutberga to marry Waldrade, but Pope Nicholas I protested. The Queen was accused of having had an incomplete sexual relationship with the King's brother, which supposedly had resulted in a pregnancy without her losing her virginity. Archbishop Hincmar of Rheims, although a defender of the absolute indissolubility of marriage, opposed the divorce chiefly because the strict rules of judicial procedure had been neglected, and great injustice had been done to the Queen. It was actually a question of the possible invalidity of marriage from the very beginning because of incestuous affinity.

1. See *ibid.*, pp. 54–157.

(4) Henry IV (1050–1108), Roman-German Emperor, wished to divorce his queen, Bertha of Turin. Alexander II (1061–1073) sent St. Peter Damiani as legate to the Imperial Diet at Frankfurt (1069) to threaten the Emperor with excommunication and exclusion from the imperial throne if he should carry out his intention.

(5) Philip August, King of France (1165–1223), in 1193 married Ingeburga of Denmark, but repudiated her immediately, and married Agnes of Meran. Innocent III (1198–1216) —repeating what Celestine III (1191–1198) had demanded —annulled the divorce sentence pronounced by an assembly of barons and bishops on account of alleged relationship in a prohibited degree. After the death of Agnes, Philip August in 1213 reinstated Ingeburga as queen.

In summarizing the events accompanying these altercations, we can say:

(1) In all these instances patent injustice had been done to the above queens, chiefly for political motives. Also, the opposition of the popes was influenced by political considerations.[2]

(2) There was no question of adultery, and the denial of popes to permit divorce does not mean necessarily exclusion of this divorce ground.

2. For example, the opposition of Pope Stephen III to Charlemagne's divorce. The true motives of the pope can be seen from his letter to Charlemagne and Carloman, when he first heard of the proposal that one of the brothers should tie the Langobards to the Franks by a marriage to Princess Desiderata. The Langobards were at the time the greatest menace to the papal possessions in central Italy, and an alliance with the Franks, who had up to that time protected the Holy See against the Langobards, would have left the popes without any defense.

After reminding both brothers that they are already married, the Pope continues, "For indeed not one of your forefathers, namely, neither your grandfather, nor your greatgrandfather, but not even your own father, took a wife from another kingdom or a foreign nation. And who of your most noble family would have deigned to contaminate or commix himself with the uncouth tribe of the Langobards, and now you are to be persuaded, what God shall avert, to be defiled by this contemptible race?" (PL 89, 1254).

(3) The insistence of the popes that the queens be taken back demonstrates that they were concerned with reparation of justice, not with the defense of indissolubility, which they might have held as ecclesiastical doctrine and practice, but did not assert in these instances.

(4) The popes did not even consider the possibility of perpetual separation from bed and board as an alternative to divorce, but only the reparation of the injustice caused to the wives of these monarchs. In other words, the sole alternative to total divorce according to the present Catholic doctrine was not even discussed.

(5) Invalidity was sometimes claimed for non-existent impediments, as by Henry VIII of England in respect to Catherine of Aragon. Naturally, such a dispute did not touch the problem of whether total divorce because of adultery is possible or not.

203

BIBLIOGRAPHY

SOURCES

Capitularia Regem Francorum, ex recens. Stephani Baluzii, vol. 1 (Paris, 1772).

Codex Iuris Canonici, Pii X Pont. Max. Iussu Digestus, Benedicti PP. XV Auctoritate Promulgatus (Rome, 1917).

Collectanea S. Congregationis de Propaganda Fide seu Decreta, Instructiones, Rescripta, pro apostolicis missionibus, 2 vols. (Rome, 1907).

Conciliorum collectio regia maxima, ed. Jean Hardouin, S.J. (Paris, 1725).

Corpus Christianorum, Series Latina. CXLVIII. Concilia Galliae (A. 314-A. 506), cura et studio C. Munier (Turnholt, 1963).

Corpus Iuris Canonici, ed. E. Friedberg (Leipzig, 1879).

Corpus Scriptorum Ecclesiasticorum Graecorum (Berlin, 1897).

Denzinger-Bannwart, *Enchiridion Symbolorum* (Freiburg i. B., 1928).

Dictionnaire de Théologie Catholique (Paris, 1950).

The Documents of Vatican II, ed. W. M. Abbott, S.J. (New York, 1966).

Migne, *Patrologiae cursus completus: Series Graeco-Latina,* 161 vols. (Paris, 1857–1866). Abbreviation-*PG*

————, *Patrologiae cursus completus: Series Latina,* 221 vols. (Paris, 1844–1855). Abbreviation-*PL*.

Monumenta Germanica Historica Epist. III Epist. Merov. et Karolini aevi (Berlin, 1892).

Opera Patrum Apostolicorum, ed. Funk, vol. I (Tübingen, 1901).

Pitra, J. S., *Iuris ecclesiastici Graecorum historia et monumenta,* vol. I (Rome, 1864), vol. II (Rome 1868).

————, *Spicilegium Sollesmense,* 4 vols. (Paris, 1852–1858).

Rouët de Journel, *Enchiridion Patristicum* (Freiburg i. B., 1920).

Sacrorum Conciliorum Nova et Amplissima Collectio, ed. Mansi, 24 vols. (Graz, 1961).

Sacrosancta Concilia ad regiam editionem executa, ed. Labbe, 21 vols. (Venice, 1728–1733).

BOOKS AND ARTICLES

Abate, Antoninus, O.P., *The Dissolution of the Matrimonial Bond in Ecclesiastical Jurisprudence* (Rome, 1962).

Adolfs, Robert, O.S.A., "The Tragedy of Broken Marriages," in *Jubilee,* March, 1966, 46–48.

Alves, Joseph T., "Consequences of Marriage Breakdown," in *Marriage: A Psychological and Moral Approach,* ed. William C. Bier, S.J. (New York, 1965), pp. 201–211.

Bailey, Derrick Sherwin, *Sexual Relation in Christian Thought* (New York, 1959).

Bender, L., *De Matrimonio* (Turin, 1958).

Benedict XIV (Prosper Lambertini), *De synodo dioecesana* (Prato, 1844).

Bernard, A., Le Bras, G., and Du Passage, H., "Usure," in *Dictionnaire de Théologie Catholique,* vol. 15, cols. 2316–2390.

Bier, William C., ed., *Marriage: A Psychological and Moral Approach* (New York, 1965).

Billot, Cardinal, S.J., *De Ecclesiae Sacramentis,* vol. II (Paris, 1927).

Bouscaren, T. Lincoln, S.J., and Ellis, Adam C., S.J., *Canon Law. A Text and Commentary* (Milwaukee, 1955).

Bride, A., "Le pouvoir du Souverain Pontife sur le mariage des infidèles," in *Revue de Droit Canonique,* X–XI, Sept.–Dec., 1960, p. 98f.; March, 1961, 51–101.

Brown, Robert McAfee, "The End to False Witness: The Challenge," address before the twenty-seventh National Conference on Religious Architecture, San Francisco, April 26, 1966 (mimeographed).

Cajetan, Thomas Cardinal, O.P., *Epistolae Pauli et aliorum apostolorum ad Graecam veritatem castigatae . . . iuxta sensum litteralem enarratae* (Venice, 1531).

Cappello, Felix M., S.J., *Tractatus Canonico-Moralis de Sacramentis,* vol. V: *De Matrimonio* (Turin, 1947).

Catharinus, Ambrosius, *Adnotationes in commentaria Caietani* (Lyons, 1542).

Cavanagh, John R., "Personality Development in Marriage," in *Marriage: A Psychological and Moral Approach,* ed. William C. Bier, S.J. (New York, 1965), pp. 252–264.

Charland, R., O.P., "Le pouvoir de l'Eglise sur les liens du mariage," in *Revue de Droit Canonique,* vol. I (Strasbourg, 1966), 44–57.

Clement, Robert, S.J., "Quelques questions a propos de la tradition orientale" (Beyrut, 1963—mimeographed).

Daudet, Pierre, *L'établissement de la compétence de l'Eglise en matière de divorce et consanguinité (France, Xième-XIIième siècles)* (Paris, 1941).

Dauvillier, Jean, *Le mariage dans le droit classique de l'Eglise depuis le Décret de Gratien (1140) jusqu'à la mort de Clément V (1914)* (Paris, 1933).

Dauvillier, Jean, and De Clercq, Carlo, *Le mariage en droit canonique orientale* (Paris, 1936).

Diekamp, F., *Theologiae Dogmaticae Manuale,* vol. IV (Paris, 1934).

Drinkwater, F. H., *Birth Control and Natural Law* (Baltimore, 1965).

Dunigan, Vincent J., C.M., "Birth Control and Politics," in *The Priest,* August, 1966, 632 ff.

Dupré, Louis, *Contraception and Catholics* (Baltimore, 1964).

Encyclopedic Dictionary of the Bible, Louis F. Hartmann, C.Ss.R., ed. (New York, 1963).

Esmein, E., *Le mariage en droit canonique* (Paris, 1935, second edition revised by R. Genestal and J. Dauvillier).

Fahrner, Ignaz, *Geschichte des Unauflöslichkeitsprinzips und der vollkommenen Scheidung der Ehe im kanonischen Recht* (Freiburg i. B., 1903).

Flatten, Heinrich, *Das Aergernis der kirchlichen Eheprozesse* (Paderborn, 1965).

Freisen, E., *Geschichte des katholischen Eherechts bis zum Verfall der Glossenliteratur* (Paderborn, 1963).

Gigot, F. E., *Christ's Teaching Concerning Divorce in the New Testament* (New York, 1932).

Glick, Paul C., *American Families. A Volume in the Census Monograph Series* (New York, 1957).

Goode, William J., *After Divorce* (Glencoe, Ill., 1959).

Gunten, F. von, O.P., "La doctrine de Cajetan sur l'indissolubilité du mariage," in *Angelicum,* vol. XLIII, 1966, 62–72.

Häring, Bernard, C.Ss.R., *Marriage in the Modern World* (Westminster, Md., 1965).

Heiler, Friedrich, *Urkirche und Ostkirche* (Munich, 1937).

Hunt, Morton M., *The World of the Formerly Married* (New York, 1966).

Jacobson, Paul H., and Jacobson, Pauline F., *American Marriage and Divorce* (New York, 1959).

Joyce, George Hayword, S.J., *Christian Marriage* (London, 1948).

Kephart, William M., *The Family, Society and the Individual* (Boston, 1961).

Kéramé, Oreste, "Oecumenisme et indissolubilité du mariage," in *Le Lien* (Cario), vol. XXXI, 1966, no. 1, 19–28.

Landy, David, *Tropical Childhood. Cultural Transmission and Learning in a Rural Puerto Rican Village* (Chapel Hill, N.C., 1959).

Le Bras, G., "Penitentiels," in *Dictionnaire de Theologie Catholique,* vol. 12.

de Léry, L. C., S.J., "La dissolution du mariage et le pouvoir des clefs," in Sciences Ecclésiastiques (Montreal), 1958, 321–339.

Leys, Roger, "Is Teilhard Dangerous?", in *Theology Digest,* XIV, 1966, 34–40.

Lucknock, Herbert M., *The History of Marriage, Jewish and Christian, in Relation to Divorce and Certain Forbidden Degrees* (London, 1895).

Marongin, Antonio, "Divorzio (storia)," in *Enciclopedia del Diritto,* vol. XIII (Varese, 1964), 482–507.

Martinez, G. Garcia, "Indisolubilidad del matrimonio rato y consumado," in *Revista Española de Derecho Canonico* (Salamanca), vol. III, 1965, 481–523.

Massarello, A., *Acta Concilii Tridentini,* vol. II, p. 251.

Mayaud, J. B. M., *L'indissolubilité du mariage. Etude historico-canonique* (Strasbourg and Paris, 1952).

McAllister, Robert J., "Psychological Incompatibility," in *Marriage: A Psychological and Moral Approach,* ed. William C. Bier, S.J. (New York, 1965), pp. 185–193.

McKenzie, John L., S.J., "The Law in the New Testament," in *The Jurist,* 1966, 167–180.

McRory, Joseph Cardinal, *The New Testament and Divorce* (Dublin, 1934).

Noldin-Schmitt-Heinzel, *Summa Theologiae Moralis,* 3 vols. (Innsbruck, 1956).

Noonan, John T., Jr., *Contraception. A History of its Treatment by the Catholic Theologians and Canonists* (Cambridge, Mass., 1965).

———, *The Scholastic Analysis of Usury* (Cambridge, Mass., 1957).

O'Connor, William R., "The Indissolubility of a Ratified, Consummated Marriage," in *Ephemerides Theologicae Lovanienses,* XIII, 1963, 692–722.

Pallavicino, Pietro Sforza Cardinal, S.J., *Istoria del Concilio di Trento,* vol. II (Rome, 1857).

Palmieri, D., S.J., *Tractatus de matrimonio Christiano* (Rome, 1880).

Perrone, G., S.J., *De Matrimonio Christiano,* 3 vols. (Rome, 1858).

Pfab, Josef, *Aufhebung der ehelichen Lebensgemeinschaft nach göttlichem, kirchlichem und bürgerlichem Recht* (Salzburg, 1955).

Piolanti, Antonio, *I sacramenti* (Florence, 1956).

Plöchl, Willibald M., *Geschichte des Kirchenrechts*, 4 vols. (Vienna, 1953–1966).

van der Poel, Cornelius, C.S.Sp., with B. Peters and T. Beemer, "Co-Habitation in 'Marital State of Mind,'" in *The Homiletic and Pastoral Review*, April, 1966, 566–577.

Pospishil, Victor J., *Orientalium Ecclesiarum: The Decree on the Eastern Catholic Churches of the Second Vatican Council* (New York, 1965).

Prat, F., S.J., *Jesus Christ. His Life, His Teaching, and His Work*, 2 vols. (Milwaukee, 1950).

Rahner, Karl, S.J., *Free Speech in the Church* (New York, 1959).

Rokosvany, Augustinus de, *De matrimonio in Ecclesia catholica*, vol. II: *De indissolubilitate matrimonii* (Augsburg, 1840).

Schillebeeckx, Edward, O.P., *Marriage. Human Reality and Saving Mystery* (New York, 1965).

Schleck, Charles A., C.S.C., *The Sacrament of Matrimony. A Dogmatic Study* (Milwaukee, 1964).

Schmitz, Hermann Josef, *Die Bussbücher und die Bussdisziplin der Kirche*, 2 vols. (Düsseldorf, 1898).

Simons, Francis, "The Catholic Church and the New Morality," in *Cross Currents*, vol. XVI, no. 4, Fall, 1966, 429–435.

Souarn, R., "L'adultère et le lien du mariage d'après l'Ecriture Sainte," in *Dictionnaire de Théologie Catholique*, vol. 2, cols. 470 ff.

Tanquerey, Adolph, *Synopsis Theologiae Dogmaticae*, 3 vols. (Paris, 1930).

Thomas, John L., S.J., *The American Catholic Family* (Englewood Cliffs, N.J., 1956).

Tixeront, Joseph, *Histoire des Dogmes*, 3 vols. (Paris, 1909).

Vacant, A., "Divorce," in *Dictionnaire de Théologie Catholique,* vol. II, cols. 498–505.

Vaccari, Alberto, S.J., "Divorce in the Gospels," in *Theology Digest,* 1957, 31–33.

Vogt, Fritz, *Das Ehegesetz Jesu* (Freiburg i. B., 1936).

Yaron, R., "The Jewish Law of Divorce at the Time of the New Testament," in *Marriage Breakdown, Divorce, Remarriage. A Christian Understanding* (Toronto, 1962), pp. 55–59.

Zhishman, Josef, *Das Eherecht der orientalischen Kirche* (Vienna, 1864).

INDEX

213

Schillebeeckx, E., 50, 63, 210
Schleck, C. A., 114, 162, 210
Schmitz, H. J., 74, 197, 198, 210
Seneca, 77
Sergius, Patriarch, 110
Shammai, Rabbi, 28, 31, 32
Simons, F., 102, 105, 210
Soissons, Council of, 52, 189
Souarn, R., 23, 209
Stephen II, Pope, 52, 178
Stephen III, Pope, 52, 179, 201, 202
Suarez, 62
Sylvester II, Pope, 171

Tamassia, 107
Tametsi, 65, 72
Tanquerey, A., 17, 210
Tertullian, 143
Thalasius, 185
Theodore of Canterbury, 52, 75, 166, 167, 188
Theodoret, 50, 165
Theophylact, 173
Theutberga, 201
Thomas Aquinas, St., 25, 31
Thomas, J. L., 85, 86, 210
Tixeront, J., 157, 210
Tours, Synod of, 74, 107
Trent, Council of, 53, 54, 59, 62 ff.
Tribur, Council of, 52, 193

Trullo, Synod of, 42

Urban III, Pope, 78
Urban VII, Pope, 66

Vacant, A., 65–67, 210
Vaccari, A., 20, 210
Vannes, Council of, 51, 186
Van Rossum, 62
Vasquez, 62
Vella, D. J., 101, 189–191
Verberie, Council of, 41, 46, 52, 189
Victor of Antioch, 51, 166
Victricius, 174
Vienne, Council of, 78
Vigilius, Pope, 56
Vix Pervenit, 80
Vogt, F., 69, 211

Waldrade, 201
Wernz-Vidal-Aguirre, 43

Yaron, R., 32, 211

Zachary, St., 52, 177, 201
Zhishman, J., 56, 107, 171, 185, 211
Zoghby, E., 11, 14, 105